MACHINIST GRINDER FIRST YEAR MCQ

MACHINIST GRINDER FIRST YEAR MCQ

MANOJ DOLE

Copyright © Manoj Dole
All Rights Reserved.

Digitization is the need of the time. In the future, training in industrial training institutes will need to be conducted using online internet to make training more convenient and easy. E-books containing a set of MCQ questions will be made available to the trainees as they need to be more accustomed to the multiple choice questions MCQ to prepare for the online exams taking place in their industrial training institutes.

With all these factors in mind, Mr. Manoj Madhukar Dole Instructor, Industrial Training Institute, Satara, has written books according to the new annual system and NSQF-5 syllabus. And they've created theoretical mobile apps and blogs to make training easier, and made all these educational materials available for download on the world famous websites Google Play Store, Amazon and Apple Book Store.

The books were published by Hon'ble Joint Director Shri Rajendra Ghume Saheb Regional Office of Vocational Education and Training, Pune on 9/1/2019, at this time Shri Prakash Saigavkar Saheb Principal Government Industrial Training Institute Aundh Pune, Shri Tukaram Misal Saheb Principal Govt. Q. Sanstha Satara, Shri Sachin Dhumal Saheb District Vocational Education and Training Officer Satara, Shri Yatin Pargaonkar Saheb Principal Govt. Q. Sanstha Kolhapur, Shri Vikas Teke Saheb Inspector Vocational Education and Training Regional Office Pune, Palekar Foods Products Pvt. Ltd. Entrepreneurial Chairman of Satara Mr. Nilkanthrao Palekar Saheb, Chairman of Hira Foods Mr. Ibrahim Baba Tamboli Saheb, Mrs. Shalmali Pawar Headmaster Government Technical School Center Satara and other dignitaries were present on the occasion.

Contents

Prologue　　　*vii*

Foreword　　　*ix*

Preface　　　*xi*

Acknowledgements　　　*xiii*

1. Machinist Grinder First Year Mcq Drawings　　　1

2. Machinist Grinder First Year Mcq　　　26

Prologue

Machinist Grinder First Year MCQ is a simple e-Book for ITI Engineering Course Lift and Escalator Mechanic, First Year, Sem- 1 & 2, Revised NSQ F-5 Syllabus in 2022 It contains objective questions with underlined & bold correct answers MCQ covering all topics including all about the latest & Important about basic fitting covering components like filing, sawing, drilling, tapping, chipping, grinding and different fits,turning operations on lathe viz., plain, facing, boring, grooving, step turning, parting, chamfering, knurling and different thread cutting by setting the different parameter, mounting, balancing, dressing and truing of grinding wheel, plain and cylindrical surfaces, viz. parallel block, plain mandrel, socket, Morse taper, sleeve, Different milling operations (plain, stepped, angular, dovetail, T-slot, contour, gear) along with surface & cylindrical grinding, taper grinding, eccentric grinding, bush, square block, V-block, angle plate, re-sharpening of side & face milling cutter and lots more.

We add new question answers with each new version. Please email us in case of any errors/omissions. This is arguably the largest and best e-Book for All engineering multiple choice questions and answers.

As a student you can use it for your exam prep. This e-Book is also useful for professors to refresh material.

Foreword

Vocational education and training is imparted through the Department of Vocational Education and Training through the Department of Business Education and Business Practical to supply multi-skilled artisans in line with the rapidly growing demand in the industrial sector in the 21st century. All the occupations within the institutions are important, as the trainees from these occupations develop multi-skills as per the demands of the industry.

with the noble intention of making available MCQ e-books suitable for all businesses, considering that all the examinations in all the industries in the industrial sector are conducted online and include MCQ method questions. Mr. Manoj Madhukar Dole has written a very good e-book on MCQ method as per the new annual syllabus. This e-book will definitely be a guide for all the trainees, trainee candidates, training instructors and others concerned.

The author of the book is Mr. Manoj Madhukar Dole, Instructor Gov. ITI Satara has 17 years of training experience. Written as a new annual pattern, this e-book incorporates modern digital QR Code technology to understand the layout, simple language, and simple syntax, diagrams and videos for each subject. So I am sure that this e-book will definitely be useful for in-depth study and exam practice. The work they have done is certainly commendable.

Mr. Tukaram Misal
Principal Government Industrial Training Institute Satara.

Preface

DGET New Delhi and CSTARI Kolkata have been implementing an annual pattern for all businesses in ITI since the August 2018 session. The examination system will also be changed and it will be online from this year and since all the questions are of Objective Type (MCQ), the trainees are in dire need of in-depth study. It is with this in mind that we are delighted to present the books based on the old NIMI pattern and a complete overview of the new annual pattern, and we hope that these books will be a guide for all business directors and trainees. Is.

For writing these books, Johar Awate Saheb, Principal of ITI Akluj. Former Principal of ITI Satara Saigavkar Saheb, Assistant Director Shri Chandrakant Dhekne Saheb Regional Office of Vocational Education and Training, Pune, District Vocational Education and Training Officer Sachin Dhumal Saheb and Headmaster Government Technical School Kendra Shalmali Pawar Madam and son Adhiraj Dole, mother Kusum Dole, I am very grateful to my father Madhukar Dole and wife Ashwini Dole for their special guidance and cooperation from time to time.

Also, in a very short period of time, the book was reviewed by Shri Rajendra Ghume Saheb, Joint Director, Vocational Education and Training Regional Office, Pune, for his invaluable time in publishing the book. I am sincerely grateful for their feedback.

I am grateful to the Instructor of ITI Satara for there continuous support from the very beginning of writing the book.

From this book, I consider myself blessed to have shared my thoughts on e-learning with you. I will not claim that this book is perfect, because considering the perfection, this book is an attempt and is in its infancy. They will be valuable for improvement if they are tested and suggested.

Manoj Dole
Dated 9/1/2019

Acknowledgements

The industrial training and theoretical examination system of our industrial training institutes and these changes have been accepted by the craft instructors and the trainees. Theoretical examinations conducted in your industrial training institutes are also conducted online. Since these examinations are of multiple choice MCQ method, the trainees will need to get more practice of such questions.

With all these considerations in mind, Mr. Manoj Madhukar, Director, Dole Crafts, Katari Industrial Training Institute, Satara, has done a thorough study and with his diligent work and added his keen intellect, according to the new annual system and NSQF-5 syllabus, e-book of Katari and other machine trades. -Book) and they have created mobile apps and blogs on theoretical topics to make training easier and have made all these educational materials available for download on the world famous websites Google Play Store, Amazon and Apple Book Store. Training has been made easier by creating a print version and using advanced techniques like QR Code.

All these educational materials will definitely be a guide for all the trainees for in-depth study and for the craft instructors and other concerned who are imparting vocational training.

Machinist Grinder First Year MCQ Drawings

Online Test Exam
ITI Books
CNC Course
AutoCAD CAM
JOB & Apprentice
Online Theory
Computer Course
Trading Course
Web Designing
MSCIT Course
Shopping Business
Internet Business
Remotasks Course
Online Services
Top Sportsmans
Indian Army
Freedom Fighters
Top Scientists
Social Reformers
Motivational Speaker
Top Richest People
Join WhatsApp Group
Join Facebook Group
Like Facebook Page
PAN / Adhar / Licence
Passport

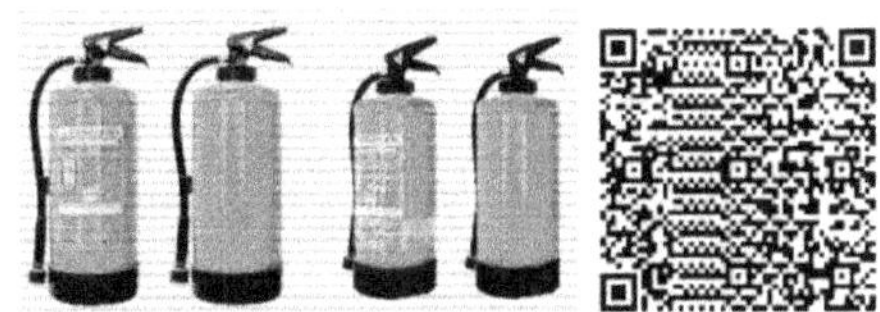
Fire extinguisher

Calliper

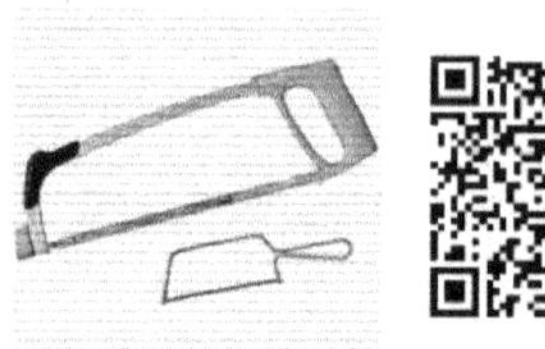

Hacksaw frame

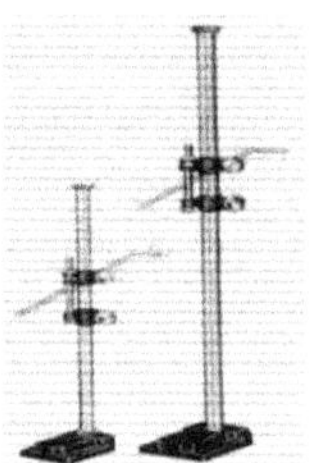

Universal surface guage

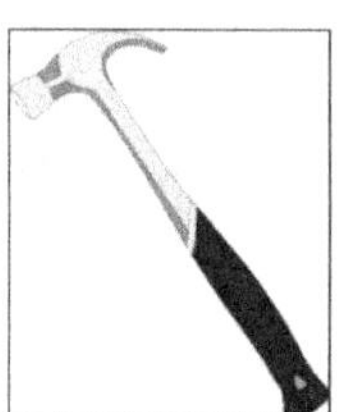

Hammer

Centre punch

Bench vice

Files

Scraper

Surface Plate

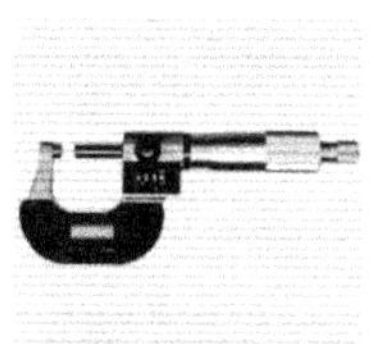

Outside Micrometer

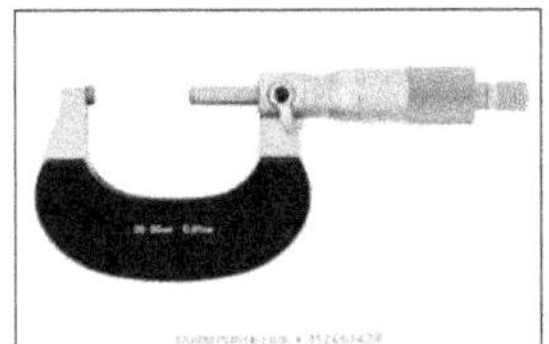

Micrometer

Depth micrometer

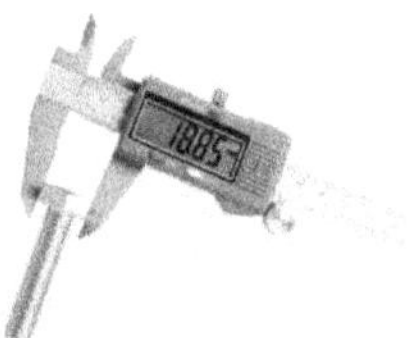

Vernier Calliper

Vernier bevel protractor

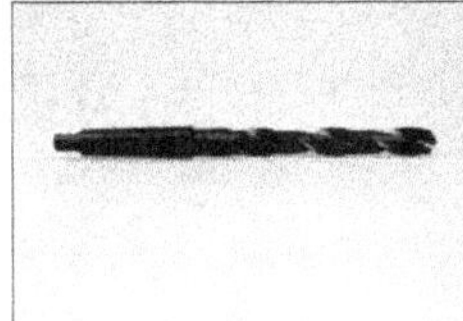

Drilling

Reamer

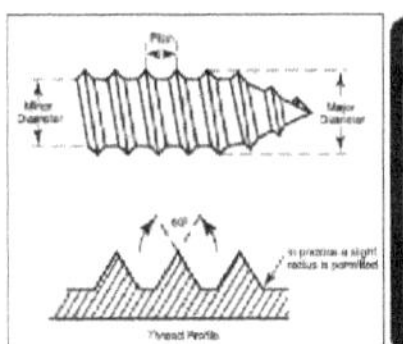

Thread

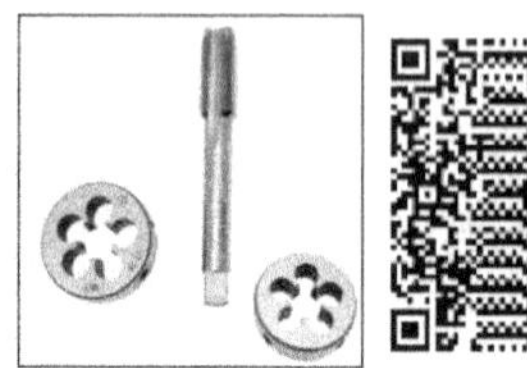

Tap Die

Grinding Wheel

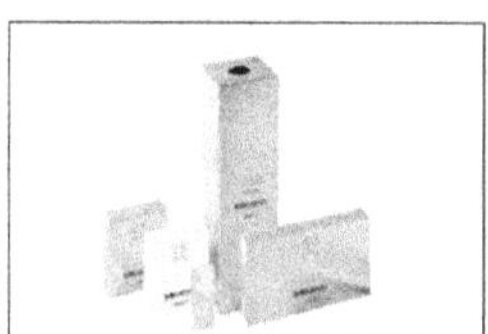

Slip gauge

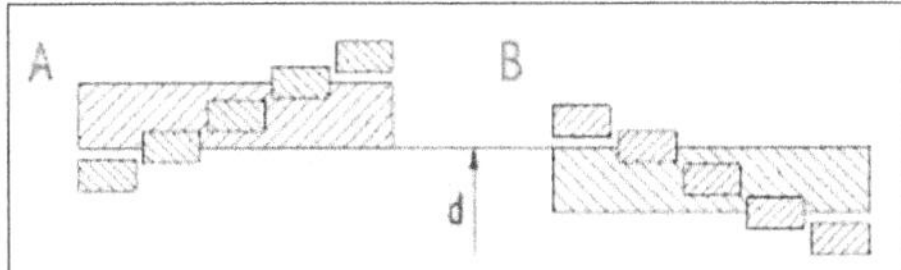

Limit fit tolerance

Lathe Machine

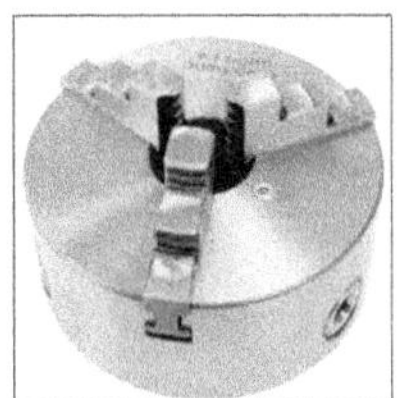

Lathe chuck

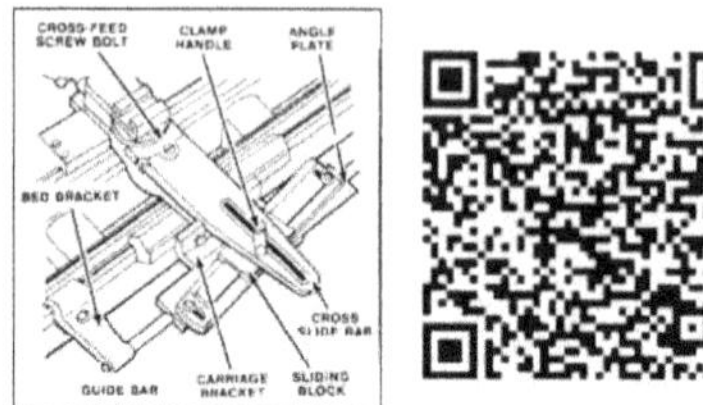

Taper turning attachment

taper ring gauge

screw pitch gauge

Gear

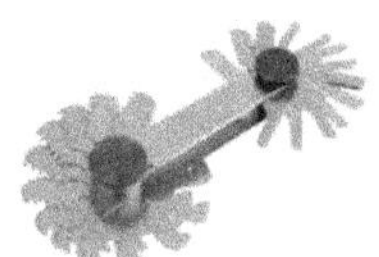

screw pitch gauge

Tap Die

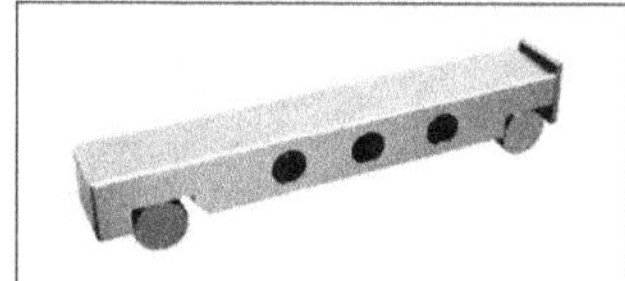

Sine bar

Slip gauge

Dial test indicator

Telescopic gauge

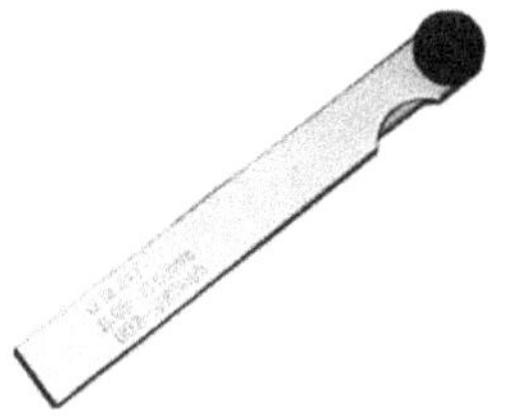 

Feeler gauge

Centre gauge

Jig

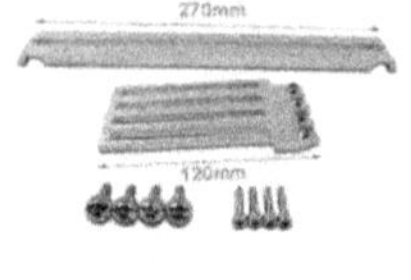

Fixture

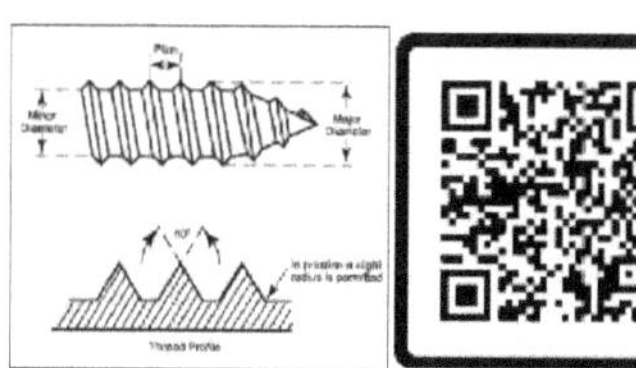

Thread

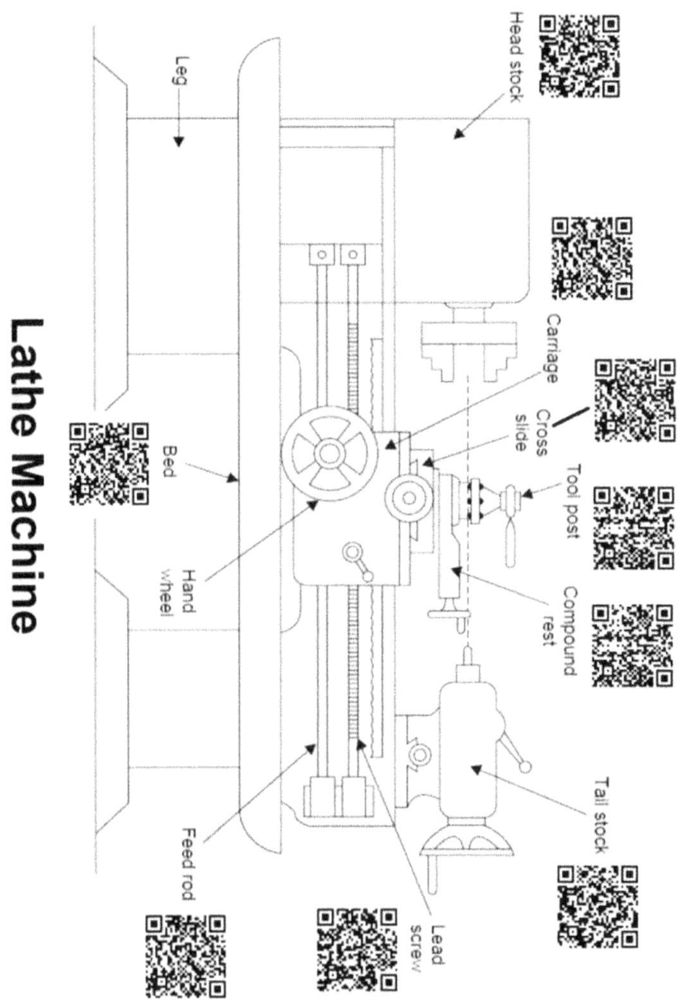
Lathe Machine
Head stock
Leg
Bed
Carriage
Cross slide
Tool post
Compound rest
Hand wheel
Tail stock
Feed rod
Lead screw

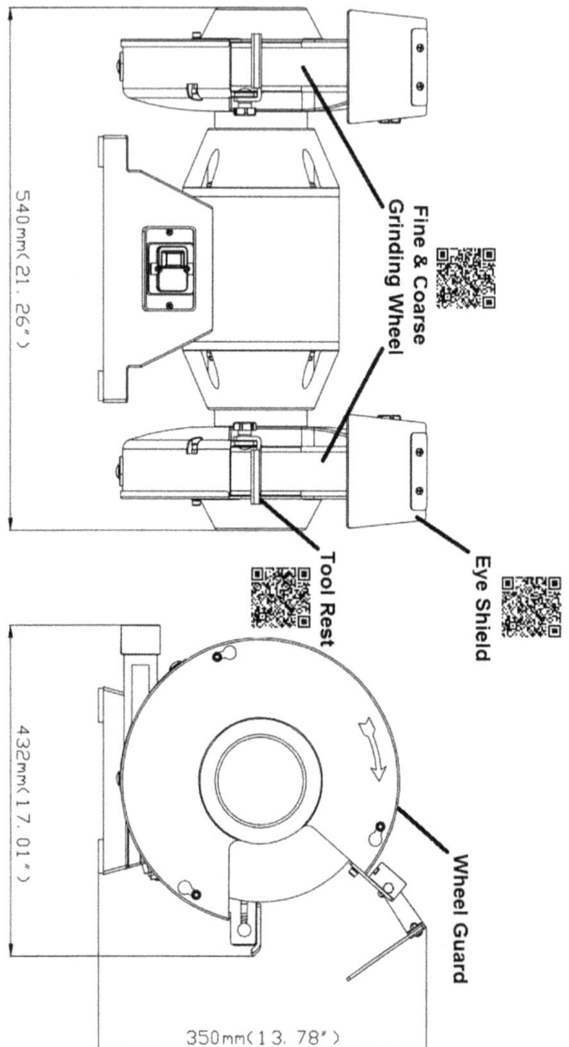

Bench Grinding Machine
Fine & Coarse Grinding Wheel
Eye Shield
Tool Rest
Wheel Guard
540mm(21.26")
432mm(17.01")
350mm(13.78")

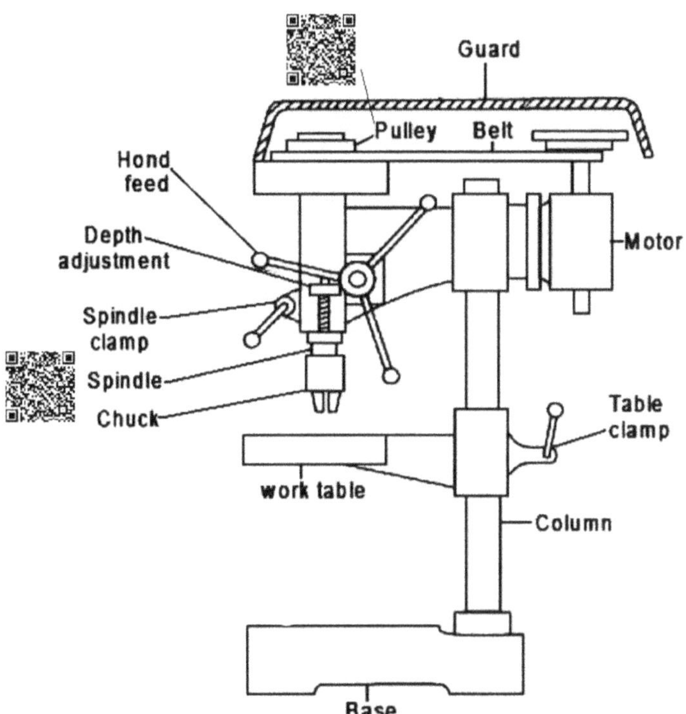

Piller Drilling Machine

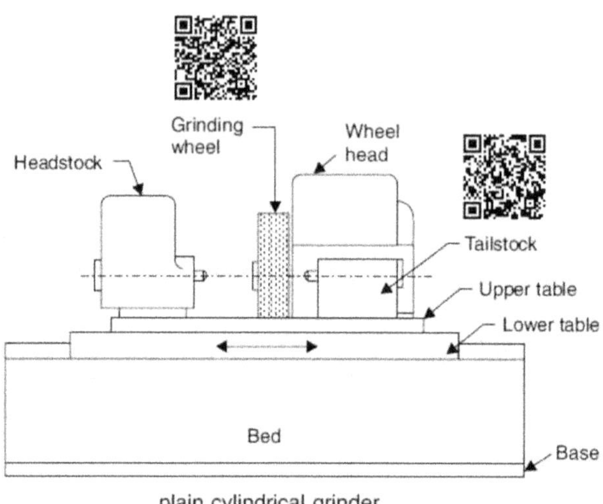

plain cylindrical grinder

Cylindrical grinding machine

To study Different operations and parts of Surface Grinding Machine

SURFACE GRINDER

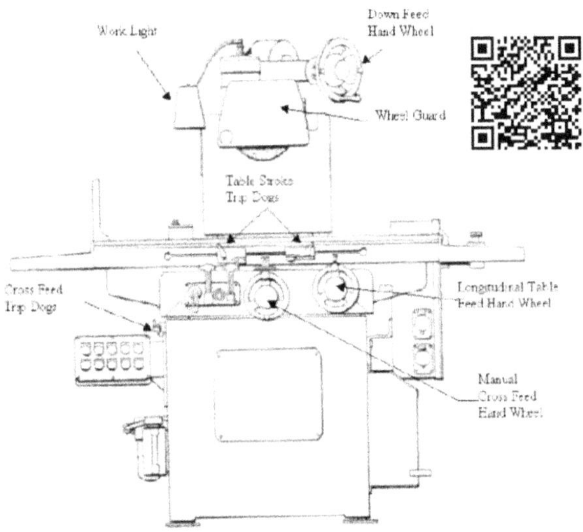

Surface grinding is used to produce a smooth finish on flat surfaces. It is a widely used abrasive machining process in which a spinning wheel covered in rough particles (grinding wheel) cuts

PLAIN OR HORIZONTAL MILLING MACHINE

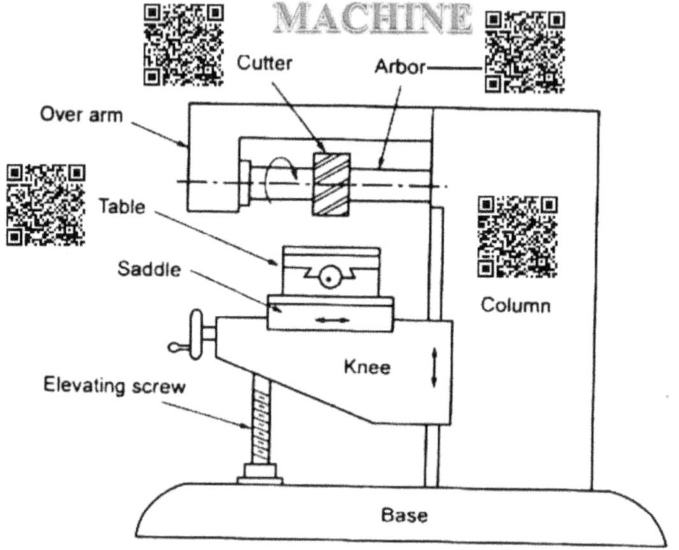

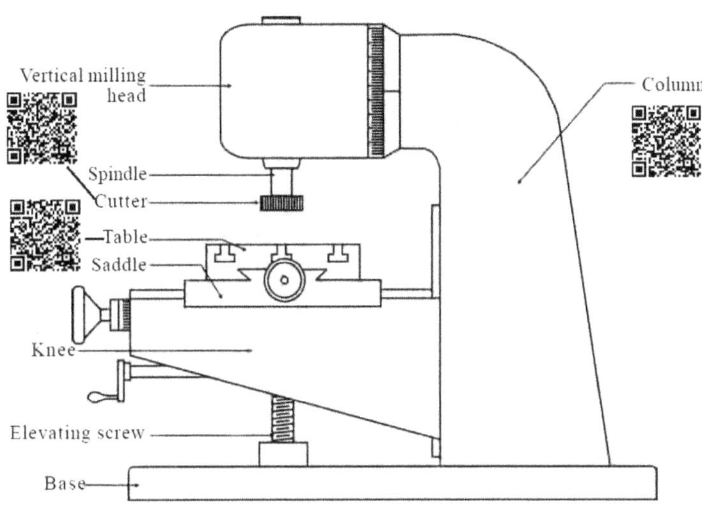

Vertical Milling Machine

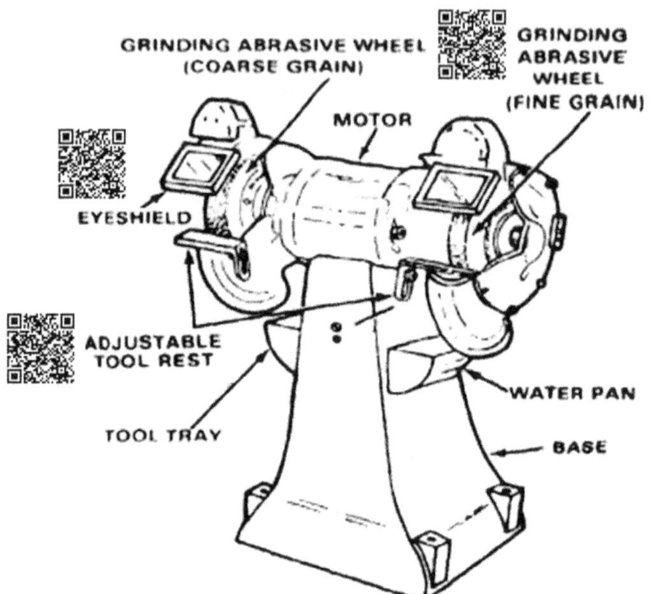

Pedastal Grinding Machine

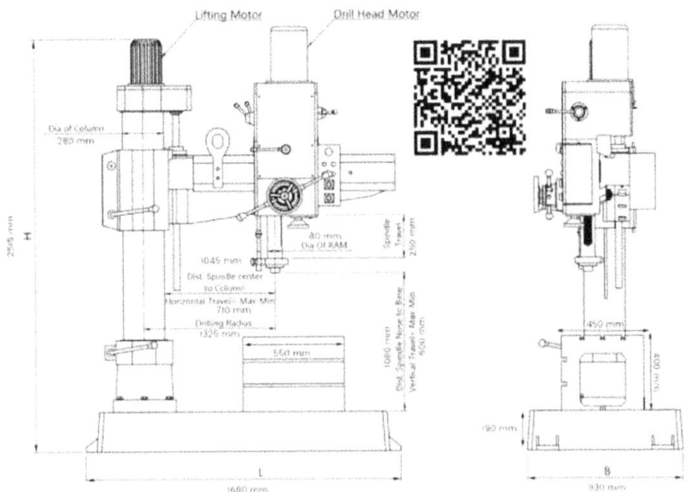

Radial Drilling Machine

CHAPTER TWO

Machinist Grinder First Year MCQ

01] While grinding, which is used to protect the eyes?
A] Dark green glass
B] Mask
C] Sun glasses
D] Safety goggles
02] In case of bleeding, take treatment Of
D] cold 3" and rest
A] spray cold water
B] Bandage immediately -----.
B] Enquire about the accident thought treatment
03] in case of an accident, the victim should im
A] Asked to take rest
C] Attended immediately
D] leave him
04] First aid is given to an injured or ill person primarily....
A] Save life
B] Prevent further deterioration of the muff's
C] Give best possible comfort
D] All of these
05] Colour code for Bins for waste paper segregation is -----
A] blue Colour
B] Yellow Colour
C] Red Colour
D] Green Colour
06] In Japanese Seiko stands for --------------
A] Shine

B] Sort

C] Standardize

D] Sustain

07] Benefit of SS system is ------

A] Increase in productivity

B] Increase in quality

C] Reduction in wastage of time

D] All of these

08] Safety is -----------

A] nobody's business

B] every bodise business

C] Some bodies business

D] The organization business

09] For basic categories of safety signs are available The meaning of"prohibition" sign ----

A] shows it must not be done

B] Shows what must be done

C] Warns the hazard or danger

D] Gives information of safety provision

10] Which one is a workshop safety?

A] Keep shop floor clean and free from grease, oil or other slippery materials

B] Stop the machine before changing the speed

C] Don't use cracked or chipped tools

D] Don't try to stop a running machine with hand

11] In Personal Protect Equipment (PPE] HELMET is used to

A] protect head

B] Protect eyes

C] Protect hands

D] Protect ears

12] Which of the following belongs to general safety?

A Have a worker in good attitude

B] The work clean and clear

C] Concentrate on your work

D] Keep the floor and gangways clean and clear

13] Which of the following is done for machine safety?

A] Check the oil level before starting the machine

B] Do things in a methodical way

C] Keep the floor and gangways clean and clear

D] Don't use dies and scarves

14] In Personal Protect Equipment (PPE], 'sleeves' is used to protect ----------

A] Face

B] Eyes

C] Ears

D] Hands

15] ABC stands for -------------

A] Automatic Breathing Control

B] Automatic Blood Control

C] Airway Breathing Circulation

D] Automatic Blood Circulation

Fire Extingusher.png

16] To put off"Class B" fire, the types of fire extinguisher used is ....

A] dry power

B] Carbon dioxide

C] Jet of water

D] Foam type

17] Which type of fire extinguisher is used to put off general fire?

A] Water type Extinguisher

B] Foam type Extinguisher

C] Dry chemical powder Extinguisher

D] Carbon dioxide (C02] Extinguisher

bench

grinder-wheel.png

18] The function of the Pedestal grinder includes ---------

A] Sharpening of the cutting tool

B] Rough grinding

C] Both (a] & (b]

D] None of these

19] The type of abrasives used for the two wheels of Pedestal Grinder are.-.

A] Coarse and Coarse type

B] Fine and fine type

C] Coarse and fine

D] None of these

20] Steel rule is a ----------

A] Marking instrument

C] Checking instrument

B] Precision instrument

D] direct measuring instrument

21] Which one of the following is a direct measuring tool?

A] Try square

B] Steel rule

C] Straight edge

22] The least count of the steel rule is..

A] 1 mm

B] 0.25 mm

C] 0.5 mm

D] 2 mm

23] The size of the dividers are specified by the -----------

A] Total length of legs

B] Distance between the points when fully opened

C] Length of legs without points

D] distance between the pivot and the point

24] The instrument used to mark parallel lines, parallel to the datum edge is -

A] jenny caliper

B] Divider

C] Outside calliper

D] Inside calliper

hand tools.png

25] Which one of the following is an indirect measuring tool?

A] Outside caliper

B] Vernier calliper

C] Steel rule

D] Outside micrometer

26] Name the punch used to locate the centre.

A] Prick punch 30°
B] Prick punch 60°
C] Centre punch
D] Dot punch

Punches.png

27] The point angle of centre punch is --------
A] 30°
B] 50°
c] 900
D] 1200
28] Different standard lengths of blade can be fitted in to..
A] Solid frame
B] Adjustable frame (flat type]
C] Fixed frame
D] Rigid frame

Hacksaw Frame
Blade.png

29] The most suitable pitch of the hacksaw blade for cutting thin. section tube is

A] 0.8 mm

B] 1.0 mm

C] 1.4 mm

D] 1.8 mm

30] Hacksaw blade teeth get dull due to ----------

C] h'gh Speed and pressure

B] Pressure not released during return stroke

A] Coolant nOt used

D] Less speed and pressure

31] Which one of the following is the standard size of Hacksaw blade?

A] 150 mm

B] 3000 mm

C] 225 mm

0] 100 mm

10] FILE 06

32] Which file used for filling wood, leather and other soft material? .

A] Single cut file

B] Double cut file

c] Rasp cut file

D] Curved cut file

Files.png

33] File used is used for ------------

A] Cleaning the work piece

C] Renewing the file teeth

B] cleaning the file teeth

D] Cleaning the chips

34] File card is used to --------

A] Clean the work piece

C] Renew the file teeth

B] Clean the file teeth

D] Clean the chips

35] The function of the Bastard file is ------

A] To reduce the material heavily

C] To file precisely

B] To remove the material rapidly

D] None of these

36] Which type if file is used for getting the material to accurate size and better finish?

A] Rough file

B] Bastard file

C] Smooth file

D] Dead smooth file

37] For filing corners and the groves with an angle more than 60° is --------

A] Round file

B] Square file

C] Triangular file
D] Knife edge file
38] The Chisels are specified according to ~-
A] Length
B] Width of chisel
C] Type of the cross section of the body
D] All of these
39] Generally the length of the handle of the vice is ----------
A] 1.5 times the normal size of the vice
B] 2.5 times the normal size of the vice
C] 3.5 times the normal size of the vice
D] 4.5 times the normal size of the vice

Bench Vice.png

40] Bench vice spindle is made of ....
A] mild steel
B] Cast iron
C] Tool steel
D] Bronze
41] The tapping drill size for M10 x 15 is --------
A] 8.2
B] 8.3
C] 8.4

<u>D] 8.5</u>

42] A nut is to be made for a screw of M10XI.S. What should be the size of drilled hole?

<u>A] 8-5 mm</u>

B] 9.0 mm

C] 9.5 mm

D] 10.0 mm

Tap Die.png

43] Tap are re-sharpened by grinding ....

<u>A] Flutes</u>

B] Threads

C] Diameter

D] Relief

44] Which size drill is used for taping width MS tap?

A] 4.5 mm

<u>B] 4.0 mm</u>

C] 0.38mm

D] 0.35mm

45] Which one of the following is used to operate form of thread by hand?

<u>A} Tap</u>

B] Threading tool

C] Threading chaser

D] Tipped tool

46] In hand tapping operation, no of taps used are ----

A] 2

B] 3

C] 4

D] 5

47] To get 100% tap in a hole the size of the hole must be equal to ----

A] Minor diameter of the tap

B] Intermediate diameter of the tap

C] Major diameter of the tap

D] None of these

48] A cutting tool used to cut outside thread is called --------

A] Drill

B] Reamer

C] Die

D] Tap

49] What coolant is recommended for taping copper or Aluminium?

A] Kerosene

B] Lard oil

C] Soda water

D] Dry air

50] The coolant used for taping copper or aluminium is --------

A] Kerosene

B] Lard oil

C] Soda water

D] Dry air

51] Lubricant is necessary to ....

A] run the machine smoothly taking least load

B] Run the machine quickly

C] Stop the machine immediately

D] Produce work piece of greater accuracy

55] Number of flutes in a twist drills are --------

A] 1

B] 2

C] 3

D] 4

56] Which one of the following drilling machines is used for drilling holes where electricity is not available?

A] Bench drilling machine

B] Pillar drilling machine

C] Redial drilling machine

D] Ratchet drilling machine

drilling

machine.png

57] Which one of the following drilling machine is used for heavy duty work?

A] Bench drilling machine

B] Pillar drilling machine

C] Radial drilling machine

D] Electric hand drilling machine

58] Drill chuck are held on the machine spindle by means of ------

A] arbor

B] Drift

C] draw-in bar

D] Chuck nut

59] Different speeds are obtained in a sensitive bench drilling machine by ----

A] Belt pulley mechanism

B] Hydraulic mechanism

C] Rack and Pinion mechanism

D] Cam and follower mechanism

60] The process of heating and cooling to change the structure of steel for obtaining the required properties is called

A] Hardening
B] Normalizing
C] Heat treatment
D] Tempering

61] The main purpose of annealing is to
A] Increase the hardness
B] Increase the toughness
C] Improve machinability
D] Improve distortion

62] The purpose of normalizing steel is to --------
A] Remove the induced Stress
B] Improve genes and reduce brittleness
C] Soften the metal
D] Increase the surface?

63] Which one of the following process is used for hardenmg the outer
5" Annealing
A] Hardening
B] Tempering
C] Case Hardening
D] Tear surface

64] The purpose of producmg a component with tough and ductIle core
and hard ou is known as......
A] Hardening
B] Case hardening
C] Tempering
D] annealing

65] Lower critical temperature of high carbon steel while hardening is
----
A] 9600C
B] 900°C
c] 7230 c
D] 56O C

66] The process of Changing the structure and thus changing the
properties by heating and 'cooling is known as --
A] Heat treatment
B] Alloying
C] Tempering
D] None of these

67] For refining the grain structure which one of the following heat treatment processes 'Is adopted.

A] Annealing

B] Hardening

C] Tempering

D] Normalising

68] Annealing is performed on iron and steel ---------

A] To remove internal stresses

B] To reduce hardness

C] To improve machinability

D] All of these

69] Which one of the following does not fall under the stages of heat treatment?

A] Heating

B] Cleaning

C] Quenching

D] Soaking

70] Gun metal is an alloy of copper, ------------

A] tin and zinc

B] Lead and zinc

C] Zinc and nickel

D] Lead and nickel

71] Cast iron is used for manufacturing machine beds because -------

A] it can resist more compressive stress

B] it is heavy in weight

C] It is cheaper metal

D] It is a brittle metal

75] Which one of the following operations can't be performed on a Center Lathe? .

A] Turning

B] Thread cutting

C] Gear cutting

D] Taper turning

76] No of gears in a Tumbler Gear unit of a lathe are ----

A] 2

B] 3

C] 4

D] 5

77] The function of a feed rod in a lathe is ----
A] To convert the rotary motion into linear motion of the tool
B] To convert the rotary motion into circular motion of the tool
C] To convert the rotary motion into circular motion of the tail stock
D] None of these
78] The use of a taper turned on lathe is ----
A] Assist to transmit drive in the assembled parts
B] Used for Assembly and disassembly of parts
C] Give self alignment in the assembled parts
D] All of these
79] Which lathe centre is used for supporting hollow end jobs?
A] Tipped centre
B] Ball centre
C] Pipe centre
D] Revolving centre
80] The included angle of live centre nose is ....
A] 30°
B] 40°
c] 500
D] 900
81] Which one of the following is used to hold the work piece for machining diameter concentric to its hole / bore?
A] Faceplate
B] Mandrel
C] Three-jaw chuck
D] Four-jaw chuck

Lathe Chuck.png

82] Which one of the following is used to hold the regular Workpice

A] Faceplate

B] Mandrel

c] Three-Jaw chuck

D] Four-Jaw chuck.

83] The threads on the back side of the four Jaw chuck has type...-----of threads.

A] Square

3] Trapezoidal

C] V -shape

D] None of these

84] The purpose of the rake angle is to --------

A] Prevent the flank of the tool rubbing with the work piece

B] guide the chips away

C] Obtain a good surface finish W

D] Increase the life of the tool

85] The angle marked"X" in the figure is a -----_ a

A] Cutting angle '

B] wedge angle

C] Front clearance angle

D] Rake angle

86] Which gauge is used to check the threading tool of lathe, for accuracy on the 60° angle?

A] Screw pitch gauge

B] Thread plug gauge

C] Centre gauge

D] Thread ring gauge

87] A hole which is not made through full depth of the component is known as --------

A] Core hole

B] blind hole

C] Pin hole

D] Bore hole

89] While drilling on lathe, the drill is held in the ------

A] Headstock

B] Tailstock

C] Compound rest

D] Bed

90] The process of enlarging the end of an existing hole to accommodate the head of socket screw is called -----------

A] Boring

B] Spot facing

C] Counter-boring

D] Counter sinking

91] The tmix-31's classified as self holding and quick releasing tapers. The self holding taper angle is

A] 3°

B] 4°

c] 5°

D] 6°

93] Which type of method is used in mass production of production of producing small length of taper?

A] Form tool

B] Compound slide

C] Tailstock offset.

D] Taper turning attachment

94] Morse standard taper is one of the internationally accepted standards taper, which is available in numbers from-------

A]1to7

B]1 to 8

C] 0 to 7

D] 0 to 8

95] Which taper turning method is used for cutting steep taper?

A] Set over method

B] Taper turning attachment

C] Form tool

D] Swivelling the compound rest

96] Morse taper is used in which of the following machine components -...

A] Spindles of lathe

B] Spindles of drill machine

C] Shanks of reamers

D] All of these

97] For mass production of the taper which one of the following method is used........

A] Tailstock offset method

B] Taper turning attachment method

C] Form too method

D] Compound slide method

98] The major diameter of the taper is 40 mm, minor diameter is 30 mm. The total length of the job is 100 mm is tapered then offset is given by

A] 5 mm

B] 7.5 mm

C] 12 mm

D] 9 mm

99] 50 metric coarse thread is designated as M12 x 125 What does '12' indicate?

A] Major diameter

B] Root diameter

C] Pitch diameter

D] Blank diameter

100] find the change gears required to cut a 3 mm pitch on 3 lat ' mm pitch 120

A] Driver / Driven =.455/120

B] Driver/ Driven = 60/120

C] Driver / Driven = 80/120

D] Driver/ Driven 2 40/80 of 5 mm

101] calculate the gears required to cut a 1 5 mm pitch on a lathe havmg lead screw Pitch

A] Driver / Driven -_20/100

B] Driver/ Driven = 30/100
C] Driver / Driven = 40/120
D] Driver/ Driven = 60/120
104] the top surface joining the two sides of adjacent thread is called
A] Crest
B] Root
C] Flank
D] Thread is angle
105] The included angle of the ISO metric thread is --------
A] 27 1 /2°
B] 30°
C] 55°
D] 60°
106] Which one of the following screw thread forms has an included angle of 55° between the flanks of threads?
A] B. A. Thread
B] Acme thread
C] Buttress threads
D] Knuckle thread
107] Which one of the following is used only for finishing and maintaining correct form of thread?
A] Tap
B] Threading tool
C] Threading chaser
D] Tipped tool
108] The angle 0f lS thread (V shaped] is ----------
A] 29°
B] 47 1/4°
C] 50°
D] 60
109] ln which of the following methods, only external threads are made --------
A] Form tool mEthOd
B] Compound rest method
C] Tailstock offset method
D] Taper turning attachment method.
110] The surface joining the crest and the root of a thread is known as ----

A] Flank
B] Shank
C] Pitch surface
D] All Of these
111] Pitch of a two start thread is 4 mm. Then the lead of the thread is given by -----
A] 4mm
B] 2mm
C] 8mm
D] 6mm
112] The Gear ratio required for cutting a screw thread of 2.5 mm on a lathe having a lead screw pitch using single point cutting tool is ----
A] 1:2
B] 2:1
C] 1:1 mm
27] Grinding
113] Grinding is a ----------
A] Single point cutting tool
B] Multi point cutting tool
C] Form tool
D] Multi point hand tool
114] The surface produced by a surface grinding is --------
A] More economical than filling
B] Less economical and more accurate
C] Less economical than filling
D] More economical and more accurate
115] Grinding is basically a ---------
A] Turning process
B] Planning process
C] Shaping process
D] Machining process
116] The scribers are made out of ----------
A] Mild steel
B] Brass
C] Cast iron
D] High carbon steel
117] The point angle of scriber is -----------
A] 30°

B] 60°

C] 5° to 10°

D] 12° to 15°

118] During marking, the reference surface id provided by -----

A] Sketch of the job

B] Work piece

C] marking off table surfaces

D] Surface gauge

Surface

Gauge.png

119] which part of a universal surface gauge

A] Fine adjusting screw

B] Guide pins

C] Base

D] R k oc er arm

120] The Operation of shaping of the grinding wheel by dressers?

A] Dressing

B] Truing

C] Clogging

D] glazing

121] Which one of the following is NOT the basic types of wheel .

A] Steel

B] Abrasive

C] Diamond

D] Boron

122] Dressing and truing of the grinding wheel are --------.

A] Exactly the same operation

B] Clone with the same equment

C] Done only for coarse grinding wheel

D] Only for form grinding

123] Accuracy or least count of a metric outside micrometric is ---------

A] 0-1 mm

B] 0.01 mm

C] 0.001 mm

D] 0.02 mm

124] 1000 microns means -----

A] 1 mm

B] 1 m

C] 1000 mm

D] 10 cm

Out Side

Micrometer.png

125] in a metric micrometer, a complete revolution of thimble advances -----------

A] 0.01 mm

B] 0.25 mm

C] 0.50 mm

D] 1.00mm

126] Ratchet Stop in the micrometer helps to ------------

A] Control the pressure

B] lock the spindle

C] Adjust the zero error

D] Hold the work piece

127] 1000 micron means ------------

A] 1 mm

B] 1 m

C] 1000 mm

D] 10 cm

128] What is the zero reading of a 50-75 mm outside micrometer?

A] 0.000 mm

B] 0.01 mm

C] 25.00 mm

D] 50.00 mm

129] The value of the smallest division on sleeve of a metric outside micrometer is -----

A] 0.50 mm

B] 1.00 mm

C] 1.50 mm

D] 2.00 mm

130] Ratchet stop in the micrometer helps to ---------

A] control the pressure

B] Lock the spindle

C] Adjust the zero error

D] Hold the work piece

131] The least count of vernier calliper is (main scale = 49 division, vernier scale = 50 division]

A] 0.1 mm

B] 0.01 mm

C] 0.001 mm

D] 0.02 mm

Vernier
Caliper.png

132] The type of measurement made by using a Vernier Calliper is -------

A] Direct measurement

B] Indirect measurement

C] 90"] (a] 81 (b]

D] None of these

133] Name the instruments shown in fig.

A] Plunger type dial test indicator

B] Lever types dial test indicator

C] Automatic type dial test indicator

D] Semi automatic type dial test indicator

Dial Guage.png

134] Name the part last bottom of Dial indicator.

A] Stem

B] Anvil

C] Plunger

D] Pointer

135] V -block and dial indicator method is used to measure the

A] Length of the work piece ground

B] Circularity of the surface of the work piece

C] Flatness of the surface

D] Pitch of the thread

136] For rough grinding which one of the following feed and work speed combinations are used?

A] Heavy feed and slow speed ,

B] Heavy feed and high speed

C] Less feed and slow speed

D] Less feed and high speed

137] Preventive maintenance is ....

A] The maintenance involves the use of sensitive instruments
B] The maintenance generally performed by operator himself
C] The work carried only when machine break down
D] plan to minimize the unforeseen break down
138] What is a break down maintenance?
A] Maintenance to minimize the unforeseen breakdown
B] Maintenance generally performed by operator himself
C] Maintenance involves replacement of worn out parts
D] Repairs work carried only when machine breakdown
139] A product is said to have the quality when ----
A] Its shape and dimensions are not within the limit
B] it is fit for use
C] It appears to be very good
D] The choice of material is right
140] The formula Name the grinding wheel shown in fig.
A] Recessed one side Type 5
B] Straight cup Type 6 .
C] Flaring cup type 7 .
D] Cylinder type 2
141] Which type of grinding wheel is used on tool and cutter grinder to sharpen the milling cutter?
A] Straight cup wheel
B] Flaring cup wheel
C] Dish wheel
D] Saucer wheel
143] Lay depends upon the method of grinding Operation Which type of grinding wheel will produce the lay shown in fig.
A] Straight wheel with reciprocating work
B] Cup wheel with reciprocating work
C] Segmental wheel on vertical spindle
D] Cup or segmental wheel with rotating work
144] Recessed on both side type grinding wheel is used to ------------
A] Change breaking
B] Grind flat surface
C] Provide clearance for the flange
D] provide clearance for both flange
145] While specifying the grinding wheel apart from the standard markings, which one of the following are mentioned -----

A] Diameter 0f the wheel
B] Thickness of the wheel
C] Shape of the wheel
D] All of these
146] The effect sing a glazed or loaded wheel is ----------
A] Less heat generation
B] Good surface finish
C] Less cutting pressure
D] excessive cutting pressure between the wheel face and the work surface
147] in a grinding operation, the ground metal particles are get clogged between the abrasive particles This is called
A] Dressing
B] Truing
C] Glazing
D] Loading
148] As During grinding the soft material particles get clogged. This is known as ~-
A] Loading
B] Glazing
C] Truing
D] Dressing
149] The soft material particles get clogged in the grinding wheel while grinding. This is called –
A] loading
B] Glazing
C] Truing
D] Dressing
150] During grinding operation, the surface of the grinding wheel develops a smooth and shining appearance. This appearance is termed as
A] Dressing
B] Truing
C] Glazing
D] Loading
151] During grinding operation, the surface of the grinding wheel develops a smooth and shining surface it is termed as ------
A] mass"
B] Wing

C] glazing
D] Loading
152] The face of a grinding wheel becomes shiny and smooth or glazed after some use The reason is.
A] Grain size is too coarse
B] grade of wheel is too hard
C] Abrasive of wheel is not suitable for the purpose
D] Structure of the wheel is too open
153] Which one of the following is not the characteristic of Glen .g Shiny
A] Blunt faced wheel
B] Wheel becoming
C] Abrasives becoming sharp
D] Wheel becoming
154] Grinding with a balanced grinding wheel will make it p05
A] dimensional accuracy with surface finish
B] Pattern Of lapsable to achieve the required ----
C] Position tolerance surface finish only
D] Positional tolerance
155] Aluminium oxide abrasive are used for grinding .
A] high tensile strength materials
B] Low tensile strength, hard and brittle materials
C] Hardened Steel
D] Cold rolled steel
156] Silicon carbide wheels are used for grinding
A] High tensile strength materials
B] low tensile strength, hard and brittle materlals
C] Hardened steel
D] Cold rolled steel
157] You have to select a grinding wheel with suitable abrasive to grind glass, What is the type of Abrasive you wili select? --------
A] Diamond
B] Emery
C] Quartz
D] Silicon carbide
158] Which among the following is an artificial abrasive?
A] Silicon carbide
B] Emery
C] Diamond

D] Corundum

159] Which type of abrasive is used for grinding carbide tipped tool?

A] Aluminium oxide

B] Silicon carbide

C] Cubic boron nitrate

D] Diamond

160] A grinding wheel marked with 'C' is made with the abrasive ------

A] Aluminium oxide

B] Silicon carbide

C] Diamond

D] Corundum

161] Which type of abrasive is used for grinding carbide?

A] Corundum

B] Tungsten carbide

C] Silicon carbide

D] Aluminium oxide

162] Which one of the following is not a natural abrasive?

A] Silicon carbide

B] Diamond

C] Emery

D] Corundum

163] As per Indian Standard, the grain size '46' comes under the group --------«

A] course

B] Medium

C] Fine

D] Very fine

165] A grinding wheel is marked as 50 A5066V7. in this 50 indicates ----

A] Type of abrasive grit

C] Grade

B] Grain size

D] Structure

166] Which one of the following factors is not considered for the selection of a grinding wheel?

A] Material to be ground and its hardness

B] Stock removal and surface finish

C] The grinding process whether wet or dry

D] Feed pre revolution

167] A grinding wheel is specified as 32 A 46 HBV what does the number 46 indicate?

A] Grade

B] Grain

C] Bond

D] Structure

168] In a standard marking system of a grinding wheel, the bond is indicated in -----

A] Position 2

B] Position 3

C] Position 4

D] posution S

169] The terms associated with grinding wheel are AA or C, that refers ---------

A] Grade

B] Bond

C] Abrasive

D] Structure

44] BOND

170] The most widely used bond in grinding wheel IS

A] verified bond

B] silicate bond

C] Shellac bond

D] Rubber bond

171] Which kind of bonds are used in cut off wheel?

A] Verified bond

B] Silicate bond

C] Shellac bond

D] rubber bond

172] Which one of the following bonds is most commonly used on grinding wheels?

A] Vitrified

B] Rubber

C] Shellac

D] Silicate

173] The symbol conventionally used for resinoid bond is ---------

A] V .

B] R

C] B

D] E

174] The symbol conventionally used for resinoid bond is ----

A] V

B] R

C] B

D] E

175] Which one of the following is not the characteristic of Vitrified bond

A] High Porosity and strength re

B] Ability to resist reaction against oils, acids and water at room temperature

C] Rapid cutting action

D] High rate of stock removal

176] For grinding wheels with size higher than 90 cm, which one of the following moulding process or bond is preferred?

A] Vitrified

B] Silicate process

C] Shellac process

D] Rubber process

177] The ideal grinding will wear away ---------

A] as the abrasive particles becomes dull

B] At a predetermined rate

C] Slowly to save money

D] Fast to give better finish

178] in a grinding wheel, the strength of the bond that holds the grain in position is called

A] Grade

B] Grain

C] Bond

D] Structure

179] Which one of the following will represent the medium grade of the wheels?

A] TtoZ

B] AtoG

C] LtoO

D]PtoS

180] in a grinding wheel the amount of bond present between the abrasive grains is called
A] Grade
B] Grain
C] Bond
D] Structure
181] Which one of the following types of wheels will machine freely?
A] Close structured
B] Open structured
C] Cross structured
D] All of these
182] in grinding, the surface speed (cutting speed] is expressed in
A] mm/minute
B] mm/second
C] m/minute
D] m/second
188] Least count of depth micrometer is
A] 0.5 mm
B] 0.2 mm
C] 0.001 mm
D] 0.01 mm
189] Which one is NOT a precision grinding machine?
A] Surface grinding machine
B] Cylindrical grinding machine
C] Offohand grinding machine
D] Tool and cutter grinding machine
190] Which one of the following is the most commonly used Precision grinding machines?
A] Surface grinders
B] Tool cutter grinders
C] Cylindrical grinders
D] All of these
191] Surface grinding machine table slides over the ----------
A] 'T' __ 5.0.:
B] 'v' slot
C] 'U' slot
D] Radial slot
192] The purpose of the surface grinder is to

A] Produce curved surface

B] Produce flat surfaces

C] Produce cylindrical surface

D] Produce uneven surface

195] The cylindrical grinding produced may be .....

A] plain, cylinder and stepped

B] Plan, tapered and cylinder

C] Cylinder, tapered and stepped

196] For grinding gear teeth, threads and splined shafts which one of the following grinding operations is preferred -------

A] Surface grinding

B] Form grinding

C] External cylindrical grinder

D] Internal grinder

197] Lapping compound material is ----------

A] Sand stone

B] Diamond

C] Quartz

D] Corundum

198] Defective work surface are produced occasionally by surface grinding machine, what may be the causes for chatter marks on the work piece?

A] Incorrect dressing

B] Coolant filter puncture

C] Too much grinding heat

D] Sufficient dressing

199] Discolouring or burnishing of work piece by grinding is due to ----------.

A] Vibration on wheel spindle

B] Improper dressing of wheel

C] Insufficient coolant

D] too much friction between work surface and wheel face

200] The glazed wheel results in

A] Poor surface finish

C] Burning of the ground surface

B] More heat generated

D] All of these

201] When tolerance given in one side of the basic dimension, it is called ---------

A].Tolerance system
B] Unilateral tolerance
C] Bilateral tolerance
D] Allowance System

202] A dimension is stated as (025 H7 in a drawing. The lower limit is -----------

A] 24.75 mm
B] 24.85 mm
C] 25.00 mm
D] 25-021 mm

203] The measured Size Of the dimensions of a component as called---------

A] Basic size
B] Nominal Size
C] Allowed size
D] Actual size

204] In the drawing the dimensions of a shaft is shown 40i 0068/0042, which is the size of Shaft within the tolerance?

A] 4.0.64 mm
B] 40.042 mm
C] 40.000 mm
D] 39.998 mm

205] In Hole basic system ----------

A] The size of the shaft is made constant
B] The Size of the hole is made constant
C] Only 'allowance is given on the hole
D] The permissible tolerance are given on the hole and the Shaft

206] The Size of a component is given as 24 -0.1. What does -O.1 indicates? _

A] Upper deviation is + 0.1 mm .
B] Lower deviation is 0.0 mm
C] Fundamental deviation is 0.0 mm
D] Lower deviation is _0.1 mm

207] The tolerance of a hole iS the difference between the -------

A] Maximum hole Size and maximum Shaft size
B] Maximum hole size and maximum hole Size

C] Minimum'hole size and maximum Shaft Size

D] Minimum hole Size and minimum shaft Size

208] A hole whose lower deviation is zero is called basic hole. Which one of the following letter indicates basic hole? .

A] E

B] F

C] G '

<u>D] H</u>

209] Which one having upper deviation zero?

<u>A] Bassc Shaft</u>

B] Basic hole

C] Tolerance

D] Clearance

210] A ball bearing on a shaft is type of fit? ,

A] Clearance fit

<u>B] Driving fit</u>

C] Shrinkage fit

D] None of the above

211] Which one of the following is important factor required to achieve the interchange ability in mass production? .

A] Geometrical accuracy.

B] Standardization

<u>C] Dimensional accuracy</u>

D] Surface finish

212] In the BIS system of limits and fits, the grade of tolerance are represented by number Symbols and there are --------i

A] 14 grades of tolerance B] 16 grades of tolerance

<u>C] 18 grades of tolerance '</u>

D] 20 grades of tolerance

213] A Product is said to have the quality when ....

A] Its shape and dimensions are within the limit

<u>B] It is fit for use</u>

C] It appears to be very good

D] The choice of material is right

limit fit

tolerance.png

214] The maximum clearance required between hole'30 +0.021, 0.000 and shaft 30 -0.110, 0.143 is.

A] 0.110 mm '

B]0.131 mm

C] 0.164 mm

D] 0.143 mm

215] A dimension is stated as 25 .1002 mm in a drawing. What is the tolerance?

A] +0.02 mm'

B] +0.04 mm

C] -0.02 mm

D] 25.00 mm

216] A pin is fitted in a hole. The tolerance zone of the pin is entirely above that of hole. The fit obtained will be?

A] Clearance fit

B] Transition fit

C] Interference fit

D] Running fit

217] Interchange ability is normally applied for? _

A] Repairing of parts

B] Mass production

C] Single piece production

D] All of these

218] Tolerance is given to the part size to............

A] Production the part within the required permissible size error

B] Increase the production

C] Decrease the Production

D] Finish the components approximately

219] Which one of the following is the clearance fit under the whole basic system?

A] 20 H7/p6'

B] 2067/211

C] ZOG/gll .

D] 20H/g11.

220] The three classes of fits as per BIS system aré .... ~ .

A] Clearance fit, interference fit and transition fit

B] Medium fit, push fit and tight fit

C] Flat fit, round fit and square fit

D] 'Sliding fit ', loose fit and shrinkage fit

221] Which one of the following tolerance specifications has a maximum dimensionless than 20 mm?

A] 20 +0.2,-0.3

B] 20 320.2

C] 20 -0.2, 0.3 e

D]m 20 +500, ~03

222] Difference between the maximum and minimum limit is -~-~~~~-~~~~~ '

A] Single informant

B] Basic shaft

C] Clearance

D] Tolerance

223] A shaft 55 running freely in bush bearing the type of fit is ---------

A] Clearance fit

B] Driving plate

C] shrinkage fit

D] None of the above

224] Drm jig bushing-are generally hardened to ------------.

A] Mild steel

B] Cast iron

C] Cast steel

D] Tooi steel

Jig Fixture.png

225] Jigs is device which -------------
A] Locate the work piece
B] Holding and supporting the work piece
C] Guide the cutting tool
D] Does all the above
226] Which among the following jigs is used forllocation from a bore?
A] Plate jig
B] Solid jig
C] Post jig
D] Box jig

Jig Fixture.png

227] Fixture is a production device which --------

A] Holds and locate the work piece

B] Holds the piece

C] Chats the work piece,

D] Neither holds nor. Locates the-work piece

228] Which one of the following is used to guide tool and hold the job in mass production? '

A] Gauge.

B] Housing

C] Fixture

D] Jig

229] Which among the following is the purpose for proi/iding bushing in a drill jig?

A] For locating accurately and guiding the drill for precise drilling operation

B] For determining the size of the hole to be drilled

C] For easy drilling

D] For getting good finished surface in the drilled holes

230] Drill jig are used for? _ ,

A] Drill operations only.

B] Clamping the job for drilling

C] Drilling, Reaming, Tapping and other operations

D] Guiding the tools only

231] Which one of the following jigs consists of drill plate, which rests on the component to be drilled? . . . .

A] Solid jig .

B] Plate jig .

C] Box jig

D] Trunnion jig

232] Jig is a device which -----------

A] Locates the work piece .

B] Hold and supports the work piece and guides tool

C] Guides the cutting tool

D] Hold the cutting tool .

233] Drill jig are used for ....

A] Drilling, reaming, tapping and other allied operations

B] Drilling operations only

C] Clamping the job when drilling

D] Guiding the tool only

234] Fixture is a production device which---------: -----

A] holds the work piece '

B] Locate the work piece

C] Holds and locates the work piece

D] Neither holds nor locates the work piece

235] Which of the following statement is correct?'

A] Gauges are used to check the size

B] Template are used to chuck-the size

C] Gauges are used to measure the size

D] Gauges are used to check shape of component

236] At what standard temperature are the gauges kept in the section?

A] 100 C

B] 20° C

C] 100 F

D] 20° F

Slip Gauge.png

237] Which grade of slip gauge is generally used in workshop?
A] Grade 0
B] Grade l
C] Grade H
D] Grade 0
238] As per Indian Standards a special set gauge is used consisting of
A] 81 Pieces
B] 112 Pieces
C] 120 Pieces
D] 130 Pieces
239] The accuracy of reference gauge is
A] 0.05 mm
B] 0.01 mm
C] 0.001 .
D] 0.0001 mm
240] ln case of ant burr on slip gauge, it should be removed by
A] Filling
B] Lapping
C] Scraping
D] Grinding
241] Hardness of slip gauge should be?
A] More than 63 HRC
B] 58 HRC
C] 55 HRC
D] 50 HRC
242]------------- Slip gauge is used for Checking component within an accuracy of 0.01 mm.
A] Workshop gauge
B] Inspection gauge

C] Reference gauge

D] Ring gauge

243], -----------is used for checking accuracy of precision instrument.

A] Gauge block

B] Fader gauge

C] Sine bar

D] Plug gauge

244] Slip gauge are Cleaned before using to ensure accuracy. What medium will you use for this purpose.

A] Oil

B] Thinner

C] Carbon tetrachloride/ White petrol

D] Turpentine oil

245]To check the dimensional accuracy of identical components, a dial test indicator is set-for t 6 Size and used as a comparator. What will you use toset to the dial test indicator?

A] Dial test indicator

B] Teeter gauge

C] Slip gauge

D], surface gauge

246] A sine bar is made with four or five equally'spaced holes on its body. The purpose of these holes is to

A] Handle the sine bar easily

B] Reduce the weight of sin bar

C] Prevent distortion of the top surface of sine bar

D] Give good appearance to the sine bar

Sine Bar.png

247] A sine bar is used for
A] Measuring the diameter of holes '
B] Finding the angle of a taper job
C] Leveling the job for drilling
D] Chuckin'g the profile of a thread
248] For measuring angles using the sine bar the angle framed according to the ratio between the height of slip gauge and the
A] Height of sine bar
B] Number slip gauge
C] Length of sine bar
D] Width of sine bar
249] -----------is used for checking angle within an accuracy of 1.
A] Gauge
B] Sine bar
C] Temple
D] Telescopic gauge
250] Centre line of the contact rollers and datum surface if the sine bar are
A] Same line' '
B] Parallel
C] Inclined
D] Perpendicular
251] The sine bar is made of -.
A] High carbon steel
B] Stabilized chromium steel '

C] High speed steel

D] Nicked steel

252] A sine bar with a length of l=200mm is used to check accurately the angle of a Work piece. The angle to be checked: 250 calculate the height 'h' of the slip gauges?

A] 84.54mm

B] 83.52mm

C] 81.81mm

D] 85.52mm

253] In an adjustable snap. gauge, two adjustable jaws are provided in. .

A] Both sides

B] One side

C] One in each side

D] None of the these

254] ------------is used for checking outside dimensions Of job.

A] Ring gauge

B] Snap gauge

C] Plug gauge

D] Screw pitch gauge

255] Fixed type snap gaUges have "Go and no Go" Ends

A] Both sides

B] On either side

C] Onthe same side

D] Separately

256] "Go and no Go" size of 25 h7 snap gauge should be -'

A] 24.977mm (Go] and 25.002mm (No 60]

B] 25.002mm (Go]and 24.977mm (No 60]

C] 24.998mm (Go] and 25.023mm (No Go]

D] 25.023mm (Go] and 24.998mm (No 60]

257] The error in squareness can be accurately determined by using –

A] Try square and slip gauge

B] Try square and feeler gauge

C] Cylinder square and slip gauge

D] Bevelled edge of Try square

258] Clearance between mating parts is measured by ....

A] dial gauge

B]"Go" gauge

C] Feeler gauge

D] calliper gauge

259] ---------------is used for checking shape of component

A] Template

B] Snap gauge

C] Instrument

D] Sine bar

260] Abrasives are classifications into.............

A] Two types

B] Three types

c] One types

D] Four types

261] Grinding wheels made out of----------------- abrasive are most common because of its free and cool cutting action.

A] Aluminium oxide

B] Silicon oxide

C] Ammonium oxide

D] Carbide.

262] Which among the following abrasive is mostly used for cutting off wheels for cutting non metallic materials?

A] Aluminium oxide

B] Silicon carbide

C] Diamond

D] None of above

263] Which abrasive particle is used for grinding tungsten carbide tool insert?

A] Silicon carbide

B] A|203

C] Diamond

D] Corundum

264] Which of the following is the natural abrasive?

A] Aluminium oxide

B] Silicon

C] Boron carbide

D] Corundum

265] Which of the following is the manufactured abrasive?

A] Corundum.

B] Quartz

C] Silicon

D] Emery

266] Which abrasive particle is used for grinding steel fittings?

A] Silicon carbide

B] Aluminium oxide

C] Diamond.

D] boron oxide

267] What kind of abrasive cut of wheel should be used to cut concrete stone and masonry?

A] Silicon

B] Al203

C] Diamond grit

D] Glass

268] Aluminium oxide wheel is used for grinding ------------

A] cast iron

B] Cemented carbide.

C] HSS '

D] ceramic

269] Which one is an incorrect statement about AIZO3 grinding wheel ....

A] it is less then tough than silicon

B] It is suitable for grinding hardened steel, hard bronze steel billets etc.

C] lt is suitable for high tensile strength material

D] It is less hard then silicon

270] The bond of diamond wheel suitable for offhand grinding of the tipped tool is ....

A] Resinoid

B] Vitrified

C] Shellac

D] Metal

271] Which among the following bonds, is used commonly?

A] Vitrified bond '

B] Rubber bond

C] Shellac bond

D] Silicate bond

272] The symbol conventionally used for resinoid .bond is ~~~~~~~~

A] v

B] R f

C] B

D] E

273] In grinding practice the term "grade of wheel" refers to ---------'

A] Hardness of the abrasive used

B] Strength of the bond of the wheel

C] Finish 0f the Wheel

D] Hardness of the work pieces

274] Which bond is used in cut of wheels?

A] Rubber

B] Vitrified

C] Resirjoid

D] Shellac

275] Hardness of grinding wheel is determine by ----------

A] the resistance exerted. by the bond against grinding Stress

B] Hardness of abrasive grains

C] Hardness of bond

D] Ability to penetration

276] When it is required to run a Grinding wheel safely at very high speed, which bond should be used? "

A] Vitrified

B] Shellac

C] Silicate

D] resinoid' and rubber

277] in surface grinding what is the suitable range of grain size of the grinding wheel for general purpose surface grinding?

A] 20 to 36

B] 46 to 60

C] 80 to 120

D] 150 to 300

278] AS per Indian Standard, the grain '46'.comes under the group of «w. -----

A] Coarse

B] Medium

C] Fine

D] Very fine

279] The grit size of the abrasives used in the grinding wheel is usually specified by ----------

A] Hardness number

B] A size of wheel

C] Softness or hardness of the abrasive

D] Mesh number

280] Advance structure in grinding wheel .... '

A]'heavy cuts

B] Ductile material

C] Hard material

D] Finishing Cut .

281] A grinding wheel is marked: 51 A46L5 V~23. What dose 5 denotes?

A] Kind of bond.

B] Structure.

C] Kind of abrasive.

D] Grain size.

282]------------wheel is mainly used for rough grinding? .

A] Cylinder

B] Tapered

C] Straight

D] Dish

283] ....is used on tool and cutter Grinders mainly to sharpen milling cutters and reamers

A] Straight cup

B] Haring cup

C] Dish

D] Recessed both sides

284] The grinding Wheel employed in surface grinding operation are classified as------------

A] Plain grinding wheel

B] Cup wheel '

C] Grinding point '

D] Dished or saucer wheel

285] There are ------------main grinding operations.

A] 2

B] 4

C] 6

D] 5

286] Listed below are the terms associated with grinding wheels describes spacing grains in the wheel

A] Structure

B] Grade

C] BOHd

D] All of these

287] Which one is an incorrect statement about grinding?

A] For cutting soft materials, hard wheel is used

B] For cutting hard material, hard wheel is used

C] For soft materials dry condition is required.

D] For grinding hard material, wet condition is required

288] ln grinding operation, which grade is used for-grinding the softer material used is .....---......

A] Softer grade

B] Medium grade

C] High grade

D] Low grade

289] ln THE Operation, for grinding harder material --------------

A] softer grade is used

B] High grade is used

C] Medium grade IS used

D] Very fine grade is used

290] The recommended depth of cut for roughing is ----------mm.

A] 0.015 to 0.050

B] 0.015 to 0.030

C] 0.010 to 0.020

D] 0.020 to 0.040

291] When using a diamond wheel for cutter grinding, a wheel speed of 1600/mm is recommended. What should be the depth of cut? .

A] 0.005-0.025mm

B] 0.025-0.04mm

C] 0.04-0.05mm

D] 0.05-0.05mm

292] The abrasive cutting off machines permit the resinoid cutting off wheel to be operated at their highest efficiency and economy. This wheel is a speed of approximately

A] Below 5000 M/Min

B] Above 5000 m/min

C] Up to 2000 m/min

D] 2000 to 3000 M/Min

293] As the diameter of the work piece decreases, the spindle speed (for the same cutting speed will

A] Remains the same

B] Decreases

C] Increases

D] None of the these

294] Feed is expressed in ----------------

A] mm/revolution

B] Inch/ revolution

C] cm/ revolution

D] M/ revolution

295] Cutting Speed (V] is expressed in ------------

A] Mm/ Second

B] Mm/ minute

C] meter/ minute

D] mm/ revolution

296] For selecting Cutting of wheel, which one of the following points is considered?

A] Spindle speed to machine

B] Dry or wet

C] Material and size of stock to be removed.

D] All the above

297] The terms associated with grinding wheel, A to Z is in increasing order of hardness of-

A] Structure _

B] Grade

C] Bond.

D] Abrasive

298] Which one is a wrong statement?

A] Fine grinding wheel is used for grinding hard as well as brittle material

B] For grinding metal first safe course grain wheel is used

C] For grinding soft metal, fine grain used

D] For grinding soft & ductile material coarse grain wheel is used

299] The grit, grade and structure if grinding wheel for specific operation is based on

A] Grinding clearance

B] Spindle size of the grinder

C] Diameter of the wheel

D] speed at which the is to be used

300] The face of the wet type grinder is crowned slightly to minimize the amount of contact between the wheel and work. This reduces the possibility of the carbide tip --

A] Being damaged or destroyed by excessive heat

B] Being ground away to rapidly

C] Damaging the wheel by causing to wear of rapidly

D] Destroyed by over heat

301] it is the abrasive process to remove chatter marks, feed spirals etc –

A].Honing

B] Lapping

C] Burnishing

D] Super finishing

302] Stock removal on diameter in the super finishing process is from..

A] 0.05 to 0.075mm

B] 0.005 to 0.025mm

C] 0.02 to 0.025mm

D] 0.002 to 0.05mm

303] When does the work piece get charged with the abrasive and cut the lap?

A] The work piece is harder than the lap

B] The work piece is softer than the lap

C] The lap is softer than the work piece

D] The lap is coarser than the work piece

304] The purpose for which lapping operation are carried out ---

A] To refine surface finish.

B] To improve quality of fit

C] To improve geometrical accuracy,

D] All the above

305] The grooves are provided on the lapping plate for-----------..

A] Preventing distortion of the plate

B] Retaining lapping paste

C] Reducing friction

D] Collects the metal-chips

306] The following material is used for diamond lapping ....

A] H55

B] Copper '

C] Aluminium oxide,

D] High carbon steel

307] Which one of the following is a cold working process by which improvement of surface finish, dimensional accuracy and work hardening can be affected without removal of metal?

A] Burnishing

B] Honing

C] Lapping _

D] Super finishing

308] In the honing Process, the movement of the spindle is ---' ------------

A] Vertical and reciprocating

B] Reciprocating

C] Vertical

D] Horizontal and reciprocating

309] lt is the process carried out by using abrasive stick?

A] Lapping

B] Honing

C] Super finishing '

D] Burnishing

310] ---------is not cause for glazing of grinding wheel

A] Hard wheel in place of soft wheel

B] Higher wheel speed than recommended

C] Dirty coolant

D] Improper dressing

311] Causes of glazing of grinding wheel can be prevented by'.............

A] Setting the feed rate correctly

B] Selecting the wheel to the recommended speed i

C] Selecting soft wheel in place of hard wheel

D] Changing the heat

312] Which among the following the cause for glazing of a grinding?

A].Grain size too fine

B] Wheel is hard '

C] Wheel speed is too fast

D] 'a' and 'b' both

313] Which one the following is the effect of a glazed or loaded grinding wheel?

A] Excessive cutting pressure between the wheel face and the work surface

B] More heat generation/"N

C] Poor surface finish

D] All the above

314] Causes of glazing when wring selection of grain size, the remedies is to -------------

A] Select medium grain size wheel in place of fine grain size wheel

B] Change the coolant

C] Select soft wheel in place of hard wheel

D] Set the wheel of the recommended speed

315] It is common by observed that the face of a. grinding wheel became shining and smooth or Glazed after some Use due to one of the stated reasons given below.

A].Abrasive of wheel not suitable for the purpose

B] Grain size is too coarse

C] Structure if the wheel is too open . .

D] Grade of wheel is too hard

316] A grinding wheel is glazed due to ---------

A] wear of abrasive grains

B] Wear of bond

C] Braking of abrasive

D] Sharpening of wheel

317] When grinding wheel become loaded or glaze they must be--------

A] Balanced properly

B] Dressed

C] Aligned all wave

D] Truing

318] the Width 0f the grinding wheel for step grinding is -------mm

A] 3 .

B] 4

C] 5 .

O] 6

319] The Rim is dressed with ~-------'~-dresser .

A] Steel

B] Diamond

C] Abrasive

D] Natural abrasive

320] in surface grinding, to expose new Position to the grinding wheel, the diamond point should be' turned to ------------from its previous position

A] 50degree

B] 90 degree

C] 180 degree

D] 45 degree

321] Grinding wheel should be dressed and trued regularly to ----------
work production

A] improue

B] Reduce

C] Loss

D] Avoid

322] The process of improving action of grinding wheel is called...............

A] Dressing operation

B] Turning operation

C] Cutting operation

D] Facing operation

323] if the grinding wheels are not balanced it Will result in --------
marks on the surface leading to poor finish.

A] Chatter

B] Line

C] Dent

D] Fading

324] Grinding with a balanced grinding wheel, will make it possible to
achieve the required -----------

A] Dimensional accuracy with surface finish

B] Pattern of lay

C] Position tolerance surface finish only

D] Positional tolerance

325] Balancing of wheel is done to?

A] Make two sides of the wheel parallel

B] Make the Outside diameter concentric with the bore

C] Equalize the weight in every position of the wheel

D] None of these

326] Defective work surface (chatter marks] are produced occasionally
by surface grinding ' machine, what may be causes? -----l

A] incorrect dressing '

B] Coolant filter punchier

C] Too much grinding heat

D] None of the above

327] Chatter marks are on work piece by grinding due to -----

A] Insufficient coolant

B] Vibration on wheel spindle

C] Too much friction between work surface and wheel the face

D] The act of restoring the cutting faces of a grinding wheel

328] Defective work surface are produced occasionally by surface grinding machine. What may cause random scratches? I

A] Incorrect dressing

B] Vibration in the machine

C] Too much grinding heat.

D] Coolant filters punctured

329] Crack is developed in grinding wheel due to ------

A] Generation of heat

B] High speed

C] Slow speed

D] Hard work

330] Pedestal grinders are used for -----------

A] Heavy duty work

B] Light duty work

C] Medium work

D] Heavy and light duty work

331] Offhand grinders are fitted to a ---------grinder

A] Surface

B] Pedestal

C] Cylindrical

D] Drilling'

332] Bench grinder are used for …………

A] Heavy duty work

B] Heavy and light duty work

C] Light duty work

D] Lather work

333] Bench Grinders are fitted on a ……………

A] Base

B] Table.

C] Wheel guards

D] Conveyor

334] Surface grinding machine & it's holding devices -141i A straight Wheel With reciprocating work will produce fine -----------on the work surface

A] Straight lines

B] Curving lines

C] Concentric lines.

D] Radial lines

335] A CUP Wheel with reciprocating will produce --------------

A] Curving lines

B] Radial lines

C] Concentric lines

D] Straight lines

336] --- --------support all the other parts of the machine.

A] Saddle

B] Table

C] Base

D] Column

337] -------------is most commonly used work holding device

A] Magnetic chuck

B] Jaw

C] Clamps

D] Vice

338] in cylindrical grinding operation the work compared to grinding wheel is always rotated at

A] Slower speed

B] Faster speed

C] Same speed

D] 100 RPM more

339] A Slight taper on the full length of a long shaft mounted between center on a universal cylindrical grinder, can be grounded by ....

A] Offsetting the tail stock

B] swiveling the tableon its base

C] Swivelling the work piece .

D] Swivelling the wheel head

340] in centre type cylindrical grinding operation when the work is mounted between centre the work is rotated by -----------

A] Using a line or rotating centre in the head stock spindle

B] The frictional drive of regulating wheel

C] The same general method used to rotate wo'rk mounted between center on lathe

D] The movement of the wheel itself

341] Silicon carbide tools can be ground --------

A] Wet

B] Dry

C] Either (A] or (B] '

D] Neither (A] nor (a]

342] Grinding wheel is folded with coolant in order to ~--------

A] Remove chips

B] Remove heat

C] Clean the wheel

D] Clean machine

343] One micron is equal to -----------m m

A] 0.1

B] 0.001

C] 1

D] 0.01

344] -------------is the COFFEC'E dimension when the micrometer measures 45.54mm, if it is having a negative error of 0.02mm

A] 45.58 mm

B] 45 54 mm

C] 45.56 mm

D] 45.53 mm.

Out Side

Micrometer.png

345] When the faces of the anvil and the spindle touch each other if the Zero of the Sleeve scale coincides with the zero of the thimble scale, then it is said to be -----------

A] Positive error

B] Negative error

C] Zero error

D] No error

346] Depth bar is used for measurement of --------------

A] Height.

B] Length

C] Depth

D] Inches

Vernier Bevel

Protractor.png

347] The accuracy of an ordinary bevel protractor is --' ------------degree.

A] One

B] Three

C] Two

D] Four

348] Preventive maintenance is -------------

A] in this maintenance involves the use of sensitive instruments

B] in this maintenance is generally performed by operator himself

C] Repair work carried only performed by operator himself.

D] Planned to minimize the unforeseen breakdown

349] The Routine Maintenance is ---------

A] it is planned maintenance to minimize the unforeseen breakdown

B] This type of maintenance involves the use of sensitive instrument

C] It is repair work carried only when machine breakdowns

D] This types of maintenance is generally performed by operator himself

350] -------- type extinguisher IS easily distinguished by distinctively Shaped discharge horn

A] Dry powder

B] Carbon dioxide

C] Forum

D] Halon

351] Maximum temperature for forging H. S. S. is -------------degree.

A] 1200

B] 100

C] 1100

D] 1500

352] Main purpose Of annealing is -----------.

A] to improve machinability

B] to improve magnetism

C] to increase hardness

D] to increase toughness

353] The carbon percentage in H.S.S. tool is -------

A] 0.75 to 1.00 %

B] 1.00 to 2.00 00

C] 0.60 to 0.75 %

D] 0.02 to 0.03 %.

354] Which one of the following is the resistance of a metal to elastic deformation?

A] Ductility.

B] Strength

C] Stiffness

D] Toughness

355]-------- gear is fitted on the main spindle

A] Tumbler

B] Spindle

C] Quick change

D] Fixed stud

356] The tumbler gear unit itself consists of ....

A] Two gears

B] Four gears

C] Three gears

D] Five gears

357] The apron is bolted .to the front end of thé--------------

A] Carriage

B] Saddle

C] Tool post

D] Top slide

Lathe Chuck.png

358] Scroll & gear mechanism is employed in -----------------
A] Collette Chuck
B] Magnetic chucks
<u>C] Three jaw chucks</u>
D] Four jaw chucks.
359] ------------------is used to support lengthy works for. Carrying out lathe operations
A] Half centre
<u>B] Lathe centre</u>
C] Ball centre
D] Tipped centre
360] The size of Three jaw chuck is specified by ---------
A] The size of each jaw
<u>B] The diameter of body of the chuck</u>
C] Width of the body chuck
D] Thickness of each chuck
361] An irregular shaped work piece is turned on a Lathe. Which one of the following work holding accessories is used?
A] Two Jaw chuck

B] Three Jaw chuck

C] Driving plate

D] Face plate

362] ------------ grooves are most commonly found on pulleys driven by V belts

A] 'V' Shaped

B] Slotted Shaped.

C] Square Shaped

D] Round Shaped

363] -------------pin tapers are used in tapper pins.

A] Standard

B] Metric

C] Jarno

D] Brown and Sharpe.

364] Built up edge is formed on the cutting edge'of cutter if material to be milled is ------------

A] Tough

B] Ductile

C] Malleable

D] Soft

365] While saw milling, the maximum depth of cut. is limited to ------------times of Slitting saw thickness.

A] 3 to 4 times

B] 2 to 3 times

C] 4 to 5 times

D] 1 to 2 times

366] The purpose of rough milling is to

A] Remove smell amounts of material at high speed

B] Remove excess material in shortest possible time

C] Provide rough finish suitable for finish operation

D] Finish the surface rough

milling machine.png

367] The purpose of finish milling is to ....
A] Bring the work piece to required dimension and surface finish
B] Bring the work piece to required dimension
C] Bring to the required surface dimension
D] Remove less material.
368] Round portion of the chips space of the milling cutter is called as
....
A] Corner slot
B] Fillet
C] Round edge
D} radius
369] A milling cutter should have three main properties. Which one of the following is correct?
A] Hardness, toughness and resistance to wear
B] Hardness, brittleness and resistance to wear
C] Hardness, softness and resistance to wear
D] Hardness, flexible and resistance to wear
370} The point angle for a standard drill is -------------degree .
A] 135 .
B] 60
C] 108 '

D] 118

Surface Gauge.png

371} The part of the Universal surface gauge which helps to draw a parallel line along edge is the ---------
A] Rocker arm
B] Snug
C] Fine adjustment
D] Guide pins (iii] Punch -.

Punches.png

372] Punches are used for forming --------of any shape
A] Holes

B] Mining

C] Knurling

D] Reaming

373] Surface plates are specified by their length and breadth & are in

Al decimetre

B] Cubic meter

C] Cylindrical

D] Drilling (v] Angle plate

374] To clamp the work piece against the face of an angle plate----------------are used.

A] Chuck

B] C clamps

C] Spindle

D] Vice

375] The Slot are provided on angle plate for ---------------

A] Accommodating bolts

B] Hanging with hooks

C] Reducing weight

D] Aligning the work

376] The size of hammer is stated by its ----------

A] Weight.

B] length

C] Shape

D] Breadth

Hammers.png

377] A short reamer with an axial hole used with an arbor or mandrel is called -------
A] Parallel reamer
B] Adjustable reamer
C] Expansion reamer
D] Chucking reamer

Reamers.png

378] Which one of the following machine reamers is used to correct the misalignment between the reamer axis and the work axis?

A] Floating blade reamer

B] Machine jig reamer.

C] Shell reamer

D] Chucking reamer

379] Tap are resharpened by grinding -----

A] Hutes

B] Threads

C] Diameter

D] Relief

380] V block are available in grade of --------

A] 0&1

B] 1&2

C] A1&A2

D] Me

V Block.png

381] V block is used to hold round bars. it has a V groove which is usually of-------------

A] 30 degree

C] 90 degree

D]120 degree

INDUSTRIAL TRAINING INSTITUTE

Monthly Test-1, Marks- 20, Date:- _______________

(Every Question Carry Two Marks)

1-06] In Japanese Seiko stands for --------------

A] Shine

B] Sort

C] Standardize

D] Sustain

2-07] Benefit of SS system is ------

A] Increase in productivity

B] Increase in quality

C] Reduction in wastage of time

D] All of these

3-08] Safety is -----------

A] nobody's business

B] every bodise business

C] Some bodies business

D] The organization business

4-09] For basic categories of safety signs are available The meaning of"prohibition" sign ----

A] shows it must not be done

B] Shows what must be done

C] Warns the hazard or danger

D] Gives information of safety provision

5-10] Which one is a workshop safety?

A] Keep shop floor clean and free from grease, oil or other slippery materials

B] Stop the machine before changing the speed

C] Don't use cracked or chipped tools

D] Don't try to stop a running machine with hand

6-11] In Personal Protect Equipment (PPE] HELMET is used to

A] protect head

B] Protect eyes

C] Protect hands

D] Protect ears

7-12] Which of the following belongs to general safety?

A Have a worker in good attitude

B] The work clean and clear

C] Concentrate on your work

D] Keep the floor and gangways clean and clear

8-13] Which of the following is done for machine safety?

A] Check the oil level before starting the machine

B] Do things in a methodical way

C] Keep the floor and gangways clean and clear

D] Don't use dies and scarves

9-14] In Personal Protect Equipment (PPE], 'sleeves' is used to protect ----------

A] Face

B] Eyes

C] Ears

D] Hands

10-15] ABC stands for --------------

A] Automatic Breathing Control

B] Automatic Blood Control

C] Airway Breathing Circulation

D] Automatic Blood Circulation

INDUSTRIAL TRAINING INSTITUTE

Monthly Test-2, Marks- 20, Date:- ________________

(Every Question Carry Two Marks)

1-20] Steel rule is a ----------

A] Marking instrument

C] Checking instrument

B] Precision instrument

D] direct measuring instrument

2-21] Which one of the following is a direct measuring tool?

A] Try square

B] Steel rule

C] Straight edge

3-22] The least count of the steel rule is..

A] 1 mm

B] 0.25 mm

C] 0.5 mm

D] 2 mm

4-23] The size of the dividers are specified by the -----------

A] Total length of legs

B] Distance between the points when fully opened

C] Length of legs without points

D] distance between the pivot and the point

5-24] The instrument used to mark parallel lines, parallel to the datum edge is -

A] jenny caliper

B] Divider

C] Outside calliper

D] Inside calliper

6-25] Which one of the following is an indirect measuring tool?

A] Outside caliper

B] Vernier calliper

C] Steel rule

D] Outside micrometer

7-26] Name the punch used to locate the centre.

A] Prick punch 30°

B] Prick punch 60°

C] Centre punch

D] Dot punch

8-27] The point angle of centre punch is --------

A] 30°

B] 50°

c] 900

D] 1200

9-28] Different standard lengths of blade can be fitted in to..

A] Solid frame

B] Adjustable frame (flat type]

C] Fixed frame

D] Rigid frame

10-29] The most suitable pitch of the hacksaw blade for cutting thin. section tube is

A] 0.8 mm

B] 1.0 mm

C] 1.4 mm

D] 1.8 mm

INDUSTRIAL TRAINING INSTITUTE

Monthly Test-3, Marks- 20, Date:- ________________

(Every Question Carry Two Marks)

1-36] Which type if file is used for getting the material to accurate size and better finish?

A] Rough file

B] Bastard file

C] Smooth file

D] Dead smooth file

2-37] For filing corners and the groves with an angle more than 60° is ---------

A] Round file

B] Square file

C] Triangular file

D] Knife edge file

3-38] The Chisels are specified according to ~-

A] Length

B] Width of chisel

C] Type of the cross section of the body

D] All of these

4-39] Generally the length of the handle of the vice is ----------

A] 1.5 times the normal size of the vice

B] 2.5 times the normal size of the vice

C] 3.5 times the normal size of the vice

D] 4.5 times the normal size of the vice

5-40] Bench vice spindle is made of ....

A] mild steel

B] Cast iron

C] Tool steel

D] Bronze

6-41] The tapping drill size for M10 x 15 is --------

A] 8.2

B] 8.3

C] 8.4

D] 8.5

7-42] A nut is to be made for a screw of M10XI.S. What should be the size of drilled hole?

A] 8-5 mm

B] 9.0 mm

C] 9.5 mm

D] 10.0 mm

8-43] Tap are re-sharpened by grinding ....

A] Flutes

B] Threads

C] Diameter

D] Relief

9-44] Which size drill is used for taping width MS tap?

A] 4.5 mm

B] 4.0 mm

C] 0.38mm

D] 0.35mm

10-45] Which one of the following is used to operate form of thread by hand?

A} Tap

B] Threading tool

C] Threading chaser

D] Tipped tool

INDUSTRIAL TRAINING INSTITUTE

Monthly Test-4, Marks- 20, Date:- _______________

(Every Question Carry Two Marks)

1-51] Lubricant is necessary to ....

A] run the machine smoothly taking least load

B] Run the machine quickly

C] Stop the machine immediately

D] Produce work piece of greater accuracy

2-55] Number of flutes in a twist drills are --------

A] 1

B] 2

C] 3

D] 4

3-56] Which one of the following drilling machines is used for drilling holes where electricity is not available?

A] Bench drilling machine

B] Pillar drilling machine

C] Redial drilling machine

D] Ratchet drilling machine

4-57] Which one of the following drilling machine is used for heavy duty work?

A] Bench drilling machine

B] Pillar drilling machine

C] Radial drilling machine

D] Electric hand drilling machine

5-58] Drill chuck are held on the machine spindle by means of ------

A] arbor

B] Drift

C] draw-in bar

D] Chuck nut

6-59] Different speeds are obtained in a sensitive bench drilling machine by ----

A] Belt pulley mechanism

B] Hydraulic mechanism

C] Rack and Pinion mechanism

D] Cam and follower mechanism

7-60] The process of heating and cooling to change the structure of steel for obtaining the required properties is called

A] Hardening

B] Normalizing

C] Heat treatment

D] Tempering

8-61] The main purpose of annealing is to

A] Increase the hardness

B] Increase the toughness

C] Improve machinability

D] Improve distortion

9-62] The purpose of normalizing steel is to --------

A] Remove the induced Stress

B] Improve genes and reduce brittleness

C] Soften the metal

D] Increase the surface?

10-63] Which one of the following process is used for hardenmg the outer 5" Annealing

A] Hardening

B] Tempering

C] Case Hardening

D] Tear surface

INDUSTRIAL TRAINING INSTITUTE

Monthly Test-5, Marks- 20, Date:- ________________

(Every Question Carry Two Marks)

1-66] The process of Changing the structure and thus changing the properties by heating and 'cooling is known as --

A] Heat treatment

B] Alloying

C] Tempering

D] None of these

2-67] For refining the grain structure which one of the following heat treatment processes 'Is

adopted.

A] Annealing

B] Hardening

C] Tempering

D] Normalising

3-68] Annealing is performed on iron and steel ---------

A] To remove internal stresses

B] To reduce hardness

C] To improve machinability

D] All of these

4-69] Which one of the following does not fall under the stages of heat treatment?

A] Heating

B] Cleaning

C] Quenching

D] Soaking

5-70] Gun metal is an alloy of copper, ------------

A] tin and zinc

B] Lead and zinc

C] Zinc and nickel

D] Lead and nickel

6-71] Cast iron is used for manufacturing machine beds because -------

A] it can resist more compressive stress

B] it is heavy in weight

C] It is cheaper metal

D] It is a brittle metal

7-75] Which one of the following operations can't be performed on a Center Lathe? .

A] Turning

B] Thread cutting

C] Gear cutting

D] Taper turning

8-76] No of gears in a Tumbler Gear unit of a lathe are ----

A] 2

B] 3

C] 4

D] 5

9-77] The function of a feed rod in a lathe is ----

A] To convert the rotary motion into linear motion of the tool

B] To convert the rotary motion into circular motion of the tool

C] To convert the rotary motion into circular motion of the tail stock

D] None of these

10-78] The use of a taper turned on lathe is ----

A] Assist to transmit drive in the assembled parts

B] Used for Assembly and disassembly of parts

C] Give self alignment in the assembled parts

D] All of these

INDUSTRIAL TRAINING INSTITUTE

Monthly Test-6, Marks- 20, Date:- _______________

(Every Question Carry Two Marks)

1-81] Which one of the following is used to hold the work piece for machining diameter concentric

to its hole / bore?

A] Faceplate

B] Mandrel

C] Three-jaw chuck

D] Four-jaw chuck

2-82] Which one of the following is used to hold the regular Workpice

A] Faceplate

B] Mandrel

c] Three-Jaw chuck

D] Four-Jaw chuck.

3-83] The threads on the back side of the four Jaw chuck has type...-----
of threads.

A] Square

3] Trapezoidal

C] V -shape

D] None of these

4-84] The purpose of the rake angle is to --------

A] Prevent the flank of the tool rubbing with the work piece

B] guide the chips away

C] Obtain a good surface finish W

D] Increase the life of the tool

5-85] The angle marked"X" in the figure is a -----_ a

A] Cutting angle '

B] wedge angle

C] Front clearance angle

D] Rake angle

6-86] Which gauge is used to check the threading tool of lathe, for accuracy on the 60° angle?

A] Screw pitch gauge

B] Thread plug gauge

C] Centre gauge

D] Thread ring gauge

7-87] A hole which is not made through full depth of the component is known as --------

A] Core hole

B] blind hole

C] Pin hole

D] Bore hole

8-89] While drilling on lathe, the drill is held in the ------

A] Headstock

B] Tailstock

C] Compound rest

D] Bed

9- 90] The process of enlarging the end of an existing hole to accommodate the head of socket

screw is called -----------

A] Boring

B] Spot facing

C] Counter-boring

D] Counter sinking

10-91] The tmix-31's classified as self holding and quick releasing tapers. The self holding taper angle is

A] 3°

B] 4°

c] 5°

D] 6°

INDUSTRIAL TRAINING INSTITUTE
Monthly Test-7, Marks- 20, Date:- _______________
(Every Question Carry Two Marks)

1-96] Morse taper is used in which of the following machine components -...

A] Spindles of lathe

B] Spindles of drill machine

C] Shanks of reamers

D] All of these

2-97] For mass production of the taper which one of the following method is used........

A] Tailstock offset method

B] Taper turning attachment method

C] Form too method

D] Compound slide method

3-98] The major diameter of the taper is 40 mm, minor diameter is 30 mm. The total length of the

job is 100 mm is tapered then offset is given by

A] 5 mm

B] 7.5 mm

C] 12 mm

D] 9 mm

4-99] 50 metric coarse thread is designated as M12 x 125 What does '12' indicate?

A] Major diameter

B] Root diameter

C] Pitch diameter

D] Blank diameter

5-100] find the change gears required to cut a 3 mm pitch on 3 lat ' mm pitch 120

A] Driver / Driven =.455/120

B] Driver/ Driven = 60/120

C] Driver / Driven = 80/120

D] Driver/ Driven 2 40/80 of 5 mm

6-101] calculate the gears required to cut a 1 5 mm pitch on a lathe havmg lead screw Pitch

A] Driver / Driven -_20/100

B] Driver/ Driven = 30/100

C] Driver / Driven = 40/120

D] Driver/ Driven = 60/120

7-104] the top surface joining the two sides of adjacent thread is called

A] Crest

B] Root

C] Flank

D] Thread is angle

8-105] The included angle of the ISO metric thread is --------

A] 27 1 /2°

B] 30°

C] 55°

D] 60°

9-106] Which one of the following screw thread forms has an included angle of 55° between the flanks of threads?

A] B. A. Thread

B] Acme thread

C] Buttress threads

D] Knuckle thread

10-107] Which one of the following is used only for finishing and maintaining correct form of thread?

A] Tap

B] Threading tool

C] Threading chaser

D] Tipped tool

INDUSTRIAL TRAINING INSTITUTE

Monthly Test-8, Marks- 20, Date:- _______________

(Every Question Carry Two Marks)

1-111] Pitch of a two start thread is 4 mm. Then the lead of the thread is given by -----

A] 4mm

B] 2mm

C] 8mm

D] 6mm

2-112] The Gear ratio required for cutting a screw thread of 2.5 mm on a lathe having a lead screw

pitch using single point cutting tool is ----

A] 1:2

B] 2:1

C] 1:1 mm

3-113] Grinding is a ----------

A] Single point cutting tool

B] Multi point cutting tool

C] Form tool

D] Multi point hand tool

4-114] The surface produced by a surface grinding is --------

A] More economical than filling

B] Less economical and more accurate

C] Less economical than filling

D] More economical and more accurate

5-115] Grinding is basically a ---------

A] Turning process

B] Planning process

C] Shaping process

D] Machining process

6-116] The scribers are made out of ----------

A] Mild steel

B] Brass

C] Cast iron

D] High carbon steel

7-117] The point angle of scriber is -----------

A] 30°

B] 60°

C] 5° to 10°

D] 12° to 15°

8-118] During marking, the reference surface id provided by -----

A] Sketch of the job

B] Work piece

C] marking off table surfaces

D] Surface gauge

9-119] which part of a universal surface gauge

A] Fine adjusting screw

B] Guide pins

C] Base

D] R k oc er arm

10-120] The Operation of shaping of the grinding wheel by dressers?

A] Dressing
B] Truing
C] Clogging
D] glazing

INDUSTRIAL TRAINING INSTITUTE
Monthly Test-9, Marks- 20, Date:- ________________
(Every Question Carry Two Marks)

1-126] Ratchet Stop in the micrometer helps to ------------
A] Control the pressure
B] lock the spindle
C] Adjust the zero error
D] Hold the work piece

2-127] 1000 micron means ------------
A] 1 mm
B] 1 m
C] 1000 mm
D] 10 cm

3-128] What is the zero reading of a 50-75 mm outside micrometer?
A] 0.000 mm
B] 0.01 mm
C] 25.00 mm
D] 50.00 mm

4-129] The value of the smallest division on sleeve of a metric outside micrometer is -----
A] 0.50 mm
B] 1.00 mm
C] 1.50 mm
D] 2.00 mm

5-130] Ratchet stop in the micrometer helps to ---------
A] control the pressure
B] Lock the spindle
C] Adjust the zero error
D] Hold the work piece

6-131] The least count of vernier calliper is (main scale = 49 division, vernier scale = 50 division]
A] 0.1 mm
B] 0.01 mm
C] 0.001 mm

D] 0.02 mm

7-132] The type of measurement made by using a Vernier Calliper is -------

A] Direct measurement

B] Indirect measurement

C] 90"] (a] 81 (b]

D] None of these

8-133] Name the instruments shown in fig.

A] Plunger type dial test indicator

B] Lever types dial test indicator

C] Automatic type dial test indicator

D] Semi automatic type dial test indicator

9-134] Name the part last bottom of Dial indicator.

A] Stem

B] Anvil

C] Plunger

D] Pointer

10-135] V -block and dial indicator method is used to measure the

A] Length of the work piece ground

B] Circularity of the surface of the work piece

C] Flatness of the surface

D] Pitch of the thread

INDUSTRIAL TRAINING INSTITUTE

Monthly Test-10, Marks- 20, Date:- _______________

(Every Question Carry Two Marks)

1-141] Which type of grinding wheel is used on tool and cutter grinder to sharpen the milling

cutter?

A] Straight cup wheel

B] Flaring cup wheel

C] Dish wheel

D] Saucer wheel

2-143] Lay depends upon the method of grinding Operation Which type of grinding wheel will

produce the lay shown in fig.

A] Straight wheel with reciprocating work

B] Cup wheel with reciprocating work

C] Segmental wheel on vertical spindle

D] Cup or segmental wheel with rotating work

3-144] Recessed on both side type grinding wheel is used to ------------

A] Change breaking

B] Grind flat surface

C] Provide clearance for the flange

D] provide clearance for both flange

4-145] While specifying the grinding wheel apart from the standard markings, which one of the

following are mentioned -----

A] Diameter 0f the wheel

B] Thickness of the wheel

C] Shape of the wheel

D] All of these

5-146] The effect sing a glazed or loaded wheel is ----------

A] Less heat generation

B] Good surface finish

C] Less cutting pressure

D] excessive cutting pressure between the wheel face and the work surface

6-147] in a grinding operation, the ground metal particles are get clogged between the abrasive

particles This is called

A] Dressing

B] Truing

C] Glazing

D] Loading

7-148] As During grinding the soft material particles get clogged. This is known as ~-

A] Loading

B] Glazing

C] Truing

D] Dressing

8-149] The soft material particles get clogged in the grinding wheel while grinding. This is called –

A] loading

B] Glazing

C] Truing

D] Dressing

9-150] During grinding operation, the surface of the grinding wheel develops a smooth and shining

appearance. This appearance is termed as

A] Dressing

B] Truing

C] Glazing

D] Loading

10-151] During grinding operation, the surface of the grinding wheel develops a smooth and shining surface it is termed as ------

A] mass"

B] Wing

C] glazing

D] Loading

INDUSTRIAL TRAINING INSTITUTE

Monthly Test-11, Marks- 20, Date:- ________________

(Every Question Carry Two Marks)

1-156] Silicon carbide wheels are used for grinding

A] High tensile strength materials

B] low tensile strength, hard and brittle materlals

C] Hardened steel

D] Cold rolled steel

2-157] You have to select a grinding wheel with suitable abrasive to grind glass, What is the type

of Abrasive you wili select? --------

A] Diamond

B] Emery

C] Quartz

D] Silicon carbide

3-158] Which among the following is an artificial abrasive?

A] Silicon carbide

B] Emery

C] Diamond

D] Corundum

4-159] Which type of abrasive is used for grinding carbide tipped tool?

A] Aluminium oxide

B] Silicon carbide

C] Cubic boron nitrate

D] Diamond

5-160] A grinding wheel marked with 'C' is made with the abrasive ------

A] Aluminium oxide

B] Silicon carbide

C] Diamond

D] Corundum

6-161] Which type of abrasive is used for grinding carbide?

A] Corundum

B] Tungsten carbide

C] Silicon carbide

D] Aluminium oxide

7-162] Which one of the following is not a natural abrasive?

A] Silicon carbide

B] Diamond

C] Emery

D] Corundum

8-163] As per Indian Standard, the grain size '46' comes under the group --------«

A] course

B] Medium

C] Fine

D] Very fine

9-165] A grinding wheel is marked as 50 A5066V7. in this 50 indicates ----

A] Type of abrasive grit

C] Grade

B] Grain size

D] Structure

10-166] Which one of the following factors is not considered for the selection of a grinding wheel?

A] Material to be ground and its hardness

B] Stock removal and surface finish

C] The grinding process whether wet or dry

D] Feed pre revolution

INDUSTRIAL TRAINING INSTITUTE

Monthly Test-12, Marks- 20, Date:- _______________

(Every Question Carry Two Marks)

1-171] Which kind of bonds are used in cut off wheel?

A] Verified bond

B] Silicate bond

C] Shellac bond

D] rubber bond

2-172] Which one of the following bonds is most commonly used on grinding wheels?

A] Vitrified

B] Rubber

C] Shellac

D] Silicate

3-173] The symbol conventionally used for resinoid bond is ---------

A] V .

B] R

C] B

D] E

4-174] The symbol conventionally used for resinoid bond is ----

A] V

B] R

C] B

D] E

5-175] Which one of the following is not the characteristic of Vitrified bond

A] High Porosity and strength re

B] Ability to resist reaction against oils, acids and water at room temperature

C] Rapid cutting action

D] High rate of stock removal

6-176] For grinding wheels with size higher than 90 cm, which one of the following moulding

process or bond is preferred?

A] Vitrified

B] Silicate process

C] Shellac process

D] Rubber process

7-177] The ideal grinding will wear away --------

A] as the abrasive particles becomes dull

B] At a predetermined rate

C] Slowly to save money

D] Fast to give better finish

8-178] in a grinding wheel, the strength of the bond that holds the grain in position is called

A] Grade

B] Grain

C] Bond

D] Structure

9-179] Which one of the following will represent the medium grade of the wheels?

A] TtoZ

B] AtoG

C] LtoO

D]PtoS

10-180] in a grinding wheel the amount of bond present between the abrasive grains is called

A] Grade

B] Grain

C] Bond

D] Structure